FOR THE LOVE OF DOG

for the
Love of Dog

A VETERINARIAN'S TALE

KATTI STRAHSMEIER-STOLLER

The events and conversations in this book have
been set down to the best of the author's memory.

ISBN 978-1-7344277-7-6 (hardcover)
ISBN 978-1-7344277-8-3 (paperback)
ISBN 978-1-7344277-9-0 (eBook)

1st Edition

Book design by Anna Hall

*To my dad, who introduced me to dogs and
what it truly means to love a pet*

CHAPTER ONE

Love and Puppies

The first time I fell in love was in the back of a trailer park double-wide. From a living room where the floral print sofa clashed magnificently with the forest green carpeting, Julie and her doting husband greeted me in their flannels, jeans, and late-80s hairstyles. I felt welcome here, and as excited as I'd always imagined I would be when I finally met someone who would change my life forever.

"We keep 'em in the back," Julie said, flashing a quick but serious smile. She was a kind woman in her late forties, but I picked up the sense of a saleswoman's flair. "Wait'll you see 'em. They're the finest we ever had, I'd say." She paused to look back at her husband. "Wouldn't you say?"

"Oh, definitely."

"It's like I told you over the phone." She motioned for me to follow. "There's eight of 'em in all, but only two still free to claim."

She led me to an oversized pen dominating a small room off the back of the hallway. An avalanche of newspaper buried the floor, and there, churning through yesterday's news, were eight newborn English Foxhound puppies, their eyes so enormous I had a hard time keeping my balance.

When I first met Cooper, he was just a few days old, and already he stood out from his seven siblings as exactly the puppy for me. I'd been pining for a dog of my own for as long as I could remember, and here I'd found one with a sweet disposition, a playful streak, and an almost total absence of physical coordination. I'd never seen a more adorably clumsy dog. His paws were outsized and meaty, and he could never seem to get them to agree with each other about anything. I'd never been so in love.

"When can I take him home?"

• • •

Four weeks. After meeting my first great love, I would have to wait four more weeks for him to be weaned to solid food and grow strong enough for me to take him home. I passed much of that long stretch in excited anticipation. Every time his cute mug would flash into my mind, it would take all my will power to prevent myself from hopping in the car and starting the drive to the state line.

When the day came, my friend Kym joined me for the ride out to Bullock, North Carolina, with the intention of helping keep my excited energy at a manageable level. She managed the job well, and after a long, scenic, sunny drive, we finally arrived.

When I saw Cooper, I could hardly believe my eyes. "What happened to my puppy?" I asked to knowing laughter from Julie the breeder.

The last time I had stood on that property, Cooper weighed five pounds and was small enough to fit in the palm of my hand. Since then, his weight had quintupled. He planted every ounce of those twenty-five pounds straight on my chest when, tongue wagging and slobber trailing, he plowed into me, puppy-style.

"He's beautiful, Katti," Kym said.

I couldn't have agreed more.

Julie and Kym helped me guide my new best friend into the way-back of my red Jeep Cherokee, Cooper's big old paws hammering into the dirt in every direction except the one he meant to go. Then we were off, bound for our new life together.

Eager to get started, I wanted to make good time on the three-hour jaunt from Bullock back to my apartment in Blacksburg, VA. I took the first turn off the country road a little sharper than I should have. The "skitter-skitter-skitter-slam" from the way-back of the Jeep let me know I should ease up, because my puppy didn't yet have his driving legs.

Kym laughed. "He sounds like he's roller skating back there."

"Sorry, Cooper. I'll slow down, I promise."

Kym and I had formed a bond over our sore-thumb nature in the animal science major we were getting ready to complete at the end of the semester. From the very first day of freshman year, it was clear that we would be the only city girls in a program dominated by aspiring farmers. I was so urban-naïve back then that I'd never even *seen* a pair of cowboy boots in person before. Now, I would spend every class day as one of only two people not wearing them. Kym was the other. Our fellow students wanted to learn as much as they could about raising and caring for cows and chickens, but all Kym and I wanted to do was hang out with the dogs. Eventually we each decided to get ourselves a big-breed dog at roughly the same time. Kym's was a Mastiff that later would become fast friends with Cooper.

"I asked Julie all the right questions, didn't I?" As an aspiring veterinarian, I had wanted to make sure it was clear to Cooper's breeder that I knew what I was talking about when it came to a dog's wellbeing.

"You asked about hip dysplasia, right?"

"Yep." When I slid onto the interstate onramp, I did it slowly, and Cooper only skittered a little this time. It seemed to me his hips were fine.

"And you checked for a heart murmur."

I nodded.

"That was impressive, by the way," Kym said. "I think Julie was a little surprised when you did that."

"I kind of *do* know what I'm talking about, don't I?"

Kym furrowed her brow. "You met Cooper's parents and asked about any health issues in their line." She passed a long look into the backseat. As I watched the road ahead, I could feel her expression warming with admiration. "And I mean, he really is perfect."

I broke into a wide, satisfied smile. "He is, isn't he?"

This was the first time I'd had a puppy since I was six years old, and Cooper couldn't have been more handsome. Whether it was a general caregiving instinct or a boundless love for animals, I knew right then that I would do whatever it took to make him happy and keep him healthy and safe for the rest of his life, even if he never did master the fine art of keeping his balance in a moving vehicle.

"So, have you heard anything yet?"

I caught a quick glimpse of my reflection in her Ray-Bans, confirming that I looked as disappointed as I felt. "No. Nothing."

"I can't believe how long it takes."

Even though Kym hadn't joined me in the decision to apply to veterinary school, our sighs were simultaneous.

"I guess they just have a ton of applications to review," I said. "I mean, you know how many people want to get into vet school."

"Yeah," Kym said, trailing off as she turned to stare out the passenger window. "Thousands."

The truth was probably closer to *tens of thousands*. At the same time, there were only twenty-seven vet schools in the country, and each one of them accepted approximately sixty entrants every year. This meant that the vast, vast majority of aspiring veterinarians like me would be left searching for a different career path. There was also geography to consider. Admissions boards nationwide played favorites to in-state candidates, and since I'd grown up in Pennsylvania, my in-state options at places like Penn required 4.0 GPAs and perfect scores on the GRE.

I didn't have those things. So my strategy had been to fill out as many hundred-dollar applications to out-of-state schools as my college-kid income and middle-class family could afford. Now, all I could do was wait.

"Well, you'll hear something soon," Kym said.

"Yeah."

Kym must have sensed my resignation, because she switched on the radio and led me into a jam-out to one of those catchy early-2000s party-pop numbers. Cooper seemed into it too.

The drive from Bullock to Blacksburg was interesting in that you could choose from any of three equally efficient routes, all of them rural. They all involved winding highways through backwoods terrain and the scenic thick of the Appalachians. Normally I might have favored one of the more rugged of the three, but with a dog in the backseat, I'd elected for the one that took us through Roanoke and featured at least some measure of smooth interstate highway.

Three hours into the drive, when Blacksburg appeared on the horizon, I started to get all fluttery in the stomach. I had been looking forward to bringing my own puppy home for years, but now that the moment was finally in sight, I felt strangely nervous.

"What if he doesn't get along with Cody?" Cody was my roommate Sara's Jack Russell Terrier.

"Are you kidding?" Kym said. "Cody's a puppy too. They'll love each other."

"But what about Corkie?"

Corkie was a Yorkie who belonged to Amy, another

roommate. He was a total sweetheart, but also older and rather set in his ways, leaving his potential affection for Cooper a little more in doubt. Bringing a puppy into a new home is difficult enough at the best of times, but the thought of trying to acclimate Cooper to a house full of three other women and two other dogs was suddenly panging me with flashes of doubt. If he didn't mesh perfectly with the environment, it might lead to friction on both the dog-to-dog and roommate-to-roommate level. I figured my close friendships with Sara, Amy, and Shelbie could weather any storm, but really, who wants to deal with storms in the first place?

When we turned onto the traffic-heavy road to which my address was attached, I spotted the 7-Eleven, and then our townhouse just behind. My heart raced as we pulled into my parking lot.

Kym took off her sunglasses and gave me that wide-eyed look that says, "You ready?"

"Okay. Let's do this."

I popped the tailgate, went around to open Cooper's crate, and flailed to hook the leash to his collar. The rush of fresh air had turned him into a tornado of pent-up energy, so it was tough to get a good hold. Finally I had him, and he bounded onto the pavement. He didn't get three steps before he stopped and puppy-squatted right there in the driveway. We had stopped every forty minutes or so during the drive to let him do his business, but now he was letting loose with more urine than I'd ever seen a dog produce.

I laughed. "Thattaboy, Coop. Get it all out."

When he was done, he bounded toward my door as if he'd always known just exactly where to go. I took one last deep breath, smiled at Kym, and turned the key.

I was kind of hoping that I'd have the opportunity to acclimate Cooper to an empty house before introducing him to everyone else, but instead, we were greeted by that symphonic cacophony of giddy squeals that only a room full of young women can pull off. All three of my roommates and Cody awaited us just inside the door. I didn't see Corkie, but it didn't matter, because one playmate was plenty for Cooper. It was all I could do to get his leash unhooked before he took off in a game of chase-me with his new friend the Jack Russell.

"Oh my God," one of my roommates said.

"He's so adorable," said another.

"Just look at that face."

"And those *paws!*"

The living room was the first room inside the door, with a counter space separating it from the kitchen just beyond, and a first-floor bedroom beyond that. Cooper led Cody through all three of these rooms, the two of them squabbling and scrumming. He tripped over those lumbering mitts of his at least three times before he made it back to the front door. There, the players switched roles, and it was Cody doing the leading and Cooper the chasing. My puppy bounded after his new friend as he circled the living room to a soundtrack of five giggling women finding seats on the sofas to watch. Clumsy as he was, Cooper gave good chase—right up until Cody took to the stairs. There at the foot of the stairs, my puppy stopped, spooked.

Cody ran halfway up before turning and yapping as if calling for his new friend to follow. Cooper would have none of it. He grumbled and paced in front of the bottom step, refusing to climb.

"So, I guess you're afraid of the stairs," I said. That would make for some interesting training. And in the meantime, I would have to get used to carrying twenty-five pounds of dog-energy up the steps to my bedroom every night.

"I can't believe how big he is already," Amy said. She looked to be keeping a sharp eye out for Corkie. Cooper had already passed the Cody test, but there was still one review to go. This made Amy seem slightly on edge. I couldn't blame her. Four women, a dog, and now two puppies made for an awfully full house. Ultimately, Corkie—who was old and cranky enough not to want a puppy for a new friend—would decide that he wasn't the hugest fan of Cooper, but Amy warmed to him eventually, so it all worked out in the end.

Meanwhile, my boisterous puppy kept careening about the house, poking his head in on everything. He pawed at doors, knocked into the barstools we kept under the counter that divided the kitchen from the living room, nosed at the trash, and picked at Cody's food bowl. Then he came to a stop in front of the antique floor-length mirror by the stairs and stood so still that I thought for a second maybe he'd forgotten how to move. He stared at himself as if awed by his own presence.

"Hey you!" I called out to him in the cartoonish voice I reserve for dogs.

That seemed to catch his attention. He finally tore away from his reflection, ran into the bedroom for a second, and then romped back into the living room. He was carrying something we couldn't identify at first. Then he turned proudly to show it to us. Someone had left a lacy pair of underwear lying on the bedroom floor, and now it was Cooper's trophy. We all hooted and laughed as we took turns trying to wrench it away from him. His jaws held tight and the slobber trailed everywhere as he ratcheted his head from side to side, the underwear smacking him cheek to cheek with each rotation. By the time we got him pinned and the underwear freed, we were all roiling with laughter.

Cooper just lay there, panting and smiling, a dog very much at home.

Then he got up and peed beside one of the barstools.

"Oh, Coop," I groaned. "How could you possibly still have to go?" I opened the front door, led him outside, and informed him that this is where we go now. He trotted onto the grass with all the grace of a show dog, his head held high as any aristocrat. He might have been a little rough around the edges, but as far as puppies go, he had exceeded my expectations in every way.

Cooper spent the rest of the afternoon and much of the evening running around with Cody and trading challenges with Corkie. Then he had finally spent all his energy and collapsed in the space between our couches. By then, my roommates and I had gotten around to drinking and chatting about our lives outside of puppy-dom, so it took me a while to notice that Cooper wasn't sleeping alone. Cody, all five pounds of him to Cooper's twenty-five, had nestled into the gap between my puppy's front and hind legs.

"Our dogs are spooning," I squeaked to Sara.

We all tumbled into a Friday-night-sitcom-grade "awwww."

Exhaustion came to me so suddenly that I almost fell asleep on the couch. I caught myself when I remembered that I had a dog to let outside and then carry up the stairs. Under the mild chill of an early summer Appalachian night, I watched my first love relieve himself in the grass. Back inside, I took him in my arms, grunted my way up the stairs, and showed him to his bed. I opened the door of the crate, and he made no complaints about stepping inside.

Then, just before I closed the door, I did something that I would do thousands of times over the course of his remarkably eventful life: I kissed him on his head and told him I loved him.

When I slipped into the sheets that night, I did so with the knowledge that, after a decade-plus of waiting, I finally had my puppy, and he was perfect. It would take another year before I learned that life often charges a premium for that kind of thing.

CHAPTER TWO

In Training

My new best friend came into my life during a period of particularly challenging transition. If you've ever tried to train a dog, you know it can be a struggle—at least initially. Dogs desperately want to please, but at the same time, they often have no idea what you're talking about when you ask them to shift toward a behavior that doesn't come naturally. If, for as long as you've been alive, your instincts draw you toward one outcome, and now you're being told that that outcome isn't available to you, it's difficult to cope with the disappointment, and even more difficult to adapt.

The same is generally true for a young woman who has aspired to be something all her life, only to see her dream shattered by a series of disappointing letters. Cooper was still so new in the house I shared with my roommates that he still hadn't quite worked out which bowl was his, which sunny corners his new dog-friends would allow him to doze in, why it wasn't okay to go to town on perfectly good trash just *lying there* in the trash can, and how exactly to hold his bladder until the strange new woman taking care of him would open the door and let him out. And here I was, trying to teach him all these things despite being an emotional wreck myself.

I had applied to five different vet schools, following my plan to scatter my applications to five locations as varied as possible in the hopes that one of them would take. Three of the letters arrived on the same day, and they all bore the same disheartening news: I was a qualified candidate, just not quite qualified enough to attend this particular vet school. To know that you're in good company with this kind of rejection—to remember that you're one of tens of thousands of people who received a rejection letter just like the one you're holding—should be more comforting than it is. After all, it's easier to deal with getting turned away by an ultra-exclusive club than it is with a take-all-comers kind of affair. It's not like I'd been rejected for membership to a beginner's kickboxing class; I'd just lost out on an opportunity to study with fifty-nine other aspiring vets at these three particular schools. And I still had those other two applications out there. These first three letters were a setback, but hey, I still had hope.

Hope is a beautiful thing. Sometimes, though, it feels like little more than a slim life-preserver in a churning sea of doubt. During periods of transition, hope can be tough to cling to, as fleeting as a young woman's plans for the future.

The bond you tend to form with a group of women with whom you live tends to be intense, especially when you're all graduating from college at the same time. Sometimes it gets so intense that thinking about living with anyone else sounds terrifying. Other times, you get so frustrated that, for a minute anyway, packing your bags and leaving sounds like the only reasonable thing to do. But as a twenty-something undergraduate senior, the closer you get to graduation day, the more readily your experiences look like the former over the latter.

I didn't want to leave that place, and it didn't seem that any of my roommates did either. On the one hand, we wanted to cling to our old behaviors—all those late nights talking about nothing more stressful than a paper we had to write or a boy we found interesting or something vexing our dogs did—but on the other hand, we were about to dive headlong into this exciting new reality our parents kept cornily referring to as "the real world," and in that real world, we would have the opportunity to fall into *Lifetime*-special clichés like growing and bettering ourselves and becoming that person we always knew we could be. For all these reasons, watching the last days of college drift by is like watching a match burn down to your fingers. You're afraid of how the ending might hurt, but in the interim, it's all just so warm and beautiful and compelling. The only real shame is that it burns so fast.

My roommates all had jobs lined up. They knew where they were going. Meanwhile, I was still waiting on two more letters from vet schools before I could know with any certainty whether my lifelong dream would be fulfilled. It's a weird sensation, being the only directionless woman in a house full of women with plans. I guess that's part of why Cooper and I became so uncommonly close so quickly: I could talk to my roommates about what it was like to look at my graduation date and not have any idea what was going to happen, and they could listen and offer support, but they didn't really understand—not in that complete, visceral sense that only comes from living it. With Cooper, I could tell him my problems, and he didn't care. He still loved me intently. He still *knew*, with every fiber of his being, that everything would be all right. That's just how dogs do.

So there I was, trying to hide my trepidation about the future and live in the moment. And there Cooper was, trying to figure out why all these women were yelling and laughing at him at the same time. Two of my roommates were lined up on one side of the house, and I stood alone on the opposite side. We all held treats at the ready, and we all had our own ideas about what Cooper needed to do in this rousing game we called "Cooper, come!" This left Cooper standing in the middle of the house, looking confused.

Every day over the past three weeks, I'd spent some time training my new best buddy on the various behaviors a dog needs if he's going to be an agreeable friend to have around the house. He'd taken well to the potty training, much to my roommates' relief. "Sit," "stand," and "down" had gone swimmingly for him too. I could even get him to "stay" from time to time, if only until he got bored with the idea of standing around waiting for me. He had become a confident, self-assured dog who seemed to know exactly what I wanted from him. Dude just couldn't figure out how to come to you when you called him.

"Cooper, come!"

He wheeled around in my direction, panting and galloping in place, his tongue waggling through that big smile of his. I repeated the command, and he just spun around again before tearing off toward the other side of the house.

We all belted with laughter as he went to Shelbie, sitting regally in front of her, tail wagging in anticipation of a treat.

"Cooper, come!" I said again.

He looked back at me but didn't bother getting up from his seat in front of Shelbie.

More laughter. Shelbie gave Cooper a treat. I rolled my eyes.

"Cooper, come!"

Now he rose and started trotting toward me, but he only got halfway before he spun and bolted back to Shelbie. I couldn't help but join in the giggling as he took a seat at her feet again. It seemed to me that Cooper, smart as he was and dedicated as he was to learning, was as directionless as the woman trying so hard to train him.

I'd done the research. I truly wanted to do everything right. To that end, he and I worked on his training every spare moment we had. Of course, we still spent most of our free time walking, playing, and snuggling together, but we would be sure to get in at least three daily training sessions of about fifteen or twenty minutes each. My roommates would always help me whenever I asked. They would discipline him when needed, would take him out when my schedule didn't allow, and would reward him when he behaved appropriately. It was all very confusing to the other dogs in the house—particularly during our sessions of "Cooper, come!" Cody and Corkie would have to wait in their bedrooms so they wouldn't interfere with the game.

In this way, Cooper had learned all the basics, and even a few showier tricks like "high five," where he slapped his paw to my open hand, "high ten," where he repeated that same action, but with both paws at the same time," and even "kisses," where he would press his nose to mine. But he never got "Cooper, come!"

That night, just a few short weeks before graduation and the end of our time together, we tried for another fifteen minutes to get Cooper to go to where he was called. It was fifteen minutes of failure and laughter. When it was over, and since it was a listless Friday night, we let Cody and Corkie out of their bedrooms, then poured some drinks and got down to the business of dishing. We were in the midst of talking about where each of us was going to live next year when Sara remembered something.

"Oh, hey," she said, rising and going to the corner of the kitchen counter where we kept our unread mail. "I almost forgot. You got a letter from Penn."

My heart skipped as she sifted through the pile and found the letter. Then it sank as she brought it back to me. I could feel my roommates' jovial expressions melt into concern as we all had the same realization. The envelope was light. It wasn't one of those thick packets you get from a school that has accepted you. This was another rejection letter.

I tried to tell myself that it was okay. For all the reasons of geography and in-state politics—to say nothing of Penn's incredibly high standards—I had never really held out much hope for a fat envelope from Philadelphia. But it's still disheartening to be rejected, especially right there in front of your friends.

"Well," I said, unable to stop the tear from falling down my cheek, "I guess that just leaves the one."

"Oh, Katti," someone said.

And then I was surrounded by comforting arms and cooing roommates. Even Cooper seemed to pick up on my dismay; he sat in front of me and pawed at my shin. I don't remember much else about that day, other than probably quite a bit of crying. I'm sure my roommates calmed me with reminders that I still had that one application left, after all. I'm also sure that someone suggested we go out and tear up the town in an effort to forget my troubles. But I know we stayed in, and I know that only Cooper could really console me.

I don't know what that dog was all about, but he always made me feel better, always made me understand that no matter what happened in my chaotic and uncertain world, everything would be okay. I guess that's one of the truest draws to living with a dog: here is this living, breathing, loving being who counts on you to take care of him just as much as you count on him to remind you that life's really not so harsh. Whenever you feel bad about yourself or your situation, you can always go hug your dog, and he'll always make you feel better.

That night, I let Cooper sleep in my bed with me. It was a rare occasion for him back during his training days, but it would become a regular thing some years later. By the time he was full grown, all hundred pounds of him would splay out on my bed while I took to a corner and shivered from a lack of cover. That first time he slept in my bed, though, it was a much more comfortable affair, although emotionally it wasn't the greatest moment for me. I'd been crying for a while by then, and Cooper could clearly sense my heartbreak. He sidled up close to me, his paws tucked between us.

"What am I gonna do with my life, Cooper?" I said, my arms draped around his neck.

He grumbled for a second, then broke into a panting smile.

I laughed as he bathed me with puppy breath, my troubles not seeming so troubling anymore. My whole life had revolved around getting into vet school. But now I could sense that, even if it didn't work out for me this time around, as long as I had Cooper with me, I'd figure out what to do.

• • •

When graduation came, I still had no real plan for my future. On the last day we would ever live together, my roommates and I embarked on a sad sort of celebration. The three of them were all planning big moves to other parts of the country. One was going to Richmond. Another to North Carolina. All three of them had jobs and living situations to be excited about. I had a pile of five rejection letters and no plan to leave. For a while there, I'd had nowhere to go but back home to Pittsburgh. I love my parents, adore the city, and had plenty of friends awaiting me there, but that was still just about the last thing I'd wanted to do. I'd spent all this time and borrowed money on an education that was supposed to align me perfectly with vet school. Accepting even a temporary move back home felt like the most colossal of failures.

So rather than face that, I'd spent most of the month of May figuring out a backup plan. Ultimately, I decided to prolong my academic career by defaulting and applying for a master's program in poultry nutrition at Virginia Tech. I hadn't planned on staying at VT, or on studying anything other than veterinary medicine, but I figured it was better to push toward an advanced degree related to animals. At best, it would boost my qualifications and experience for the next round of vet school applications in the spring of the following year. At worst, I'd wind up with a master's in an animal-related field. That's not something for which I would have settled—I still knew that I would never allow the veterinarian dream to die—but I was at least wise enough by then to know that sometimes you just have to bide your time and take what you're given.

Even with a plan in place, I've never felt quite as alone as I did on that last night with my friends and roommates. Everybody else was moving on to what they wanted to do, and here I was staying in the same place, pursuing a degree I didn't really want. Adding insult to injury, I had to find a last-minute living situation for the summer, and the only opportunity that came up was to live in a rental house with a friend named Hannah, who, as luck would have it, had gotten into Virginia Tech's vet school. *I'm still here,* I thought darkly, a*nd everybody else is going away to do what they want.* I felt stuck, depressed, and utterly lonely.

The morning of our move, I helped my roommates pack their boxes and dogs into their cars and hugged them all goodbye.

"You'll be okay," Shelbie assured me.

I nodded into her embrace, my eyes watering again. I was getting pretty tired of crying by then, so I did my best to hold it back. Cooper, always a dog to want in on hugs, shoved himself between our legs, panting and looking up as we laughed. When Shelbie and I pulled apart, I saw that she was crying, and that was too much for me.

"Call me when you get in," I told her, the tears falling.

Shelbie nodded as she wiped at her eyes with the backs of her hands.

Cooper grumbled, then took a seat in that proud way of his.

One by one, I packed up my roommates and waved them away. When they were gone, I gathered together my own things and cleaned up the apartment. Afterward, the place looked as empty as my future felt. Cooper barked as if to say goodbye to his first real home, his voice reverberating off the empty walls. He seemed to like the effect, because he did it again, then performed a little sprint-circle around the vacant living room.

"C'mon, bum," I said. "We should get going." Don't ask me why, but I had taken to calling Cooper "bum" from time to time. I guess it's just one of those silly, love-struck things I did. Plus, it fit him like a vintage jean jacket.

With the Jeep all packed, I opened the back door and let Cooper hop into his travel crate. Then, with one last look back, I climbed into the driver's seat and headed toward a year of studying chickens.

• • •

"Wait, what?"

That was how I phrased the question to my poultry sciences professor when I learned of my first assignment on the chicken farm. I asked not because I hadn't heard or understood, but because I've never been a morning person, and my mind is often foggy at strange hours like 6am. That was my expected arrival time at the poultry farm—not the kind of hour I was used to waking, let alone to haul fifty-pound buckets of feed.

"We'll need a feed bucket at each coop," my professor repeated. "You'll find them in the barn, lined up on the western wall."

"But . . ." I was too glassy-headed to finish the sentiment.

"We can't start our measurements until we have the feed in place. This'll be the routine every morning, so get used to it."

That was my initiation into poultry science. I'd wake every morning at 5:30, throw on some boots and coveralls, check in at the farm by 6, and lug barrels of feed back and forth for hours. Then my fellow master's students and I would weigh the feed, check the health of each chicken, pick all the eggs, and chart every piece of information about feed-receiving and egg-laying we could collect. When it was done, we would transfer all the handwritten data into the computers at the lab.

"Oh, and you'll want to take that off," my professor called after me as I trudged toward the barn on Day One.

I looked back, confused.

"The bracelet." He pointed at the gift I had received from my parents as a graduation present.

With a vacant gaze, I grabbed at the bracelet and held it in my palm.

My professor gave an exasperated look. "The chickens don't like metal. If you wear that thing, they'll come after you."

When you're pursuing a master's in poultry science, you learn a number of interesting things about chickens. For me, the fact that metallic objects made them finger-biting crazy was only the first. I also learned that the color red gets them all amorous, so unless I wanted to be chicken-boned, I should leave the fall colors at home. Generally you have to watch yourself around America's favorite fowl, or you'll wind up with hands so nipped and pecked that you have to swear to friends and relatives you haven't taken up a nighttime hobby as a bare-knuckles boxer.

It wasn't all farm work in the program—just three hours of it every morning. At 9am, classes would start. Each would last about an hour, and they'd come up sporadically over the course of the day, just like any undergraduate or graduate program. Class sizes were small, with maybe ten to fifteen people in each session, and I'd be the only one in any given class who didn't aspire to make my living as a farmer. Just like that last day with my roommates, it seemed to me that everyone here was in the place they wanted and needed to be, while I desperately wanted to be somewhere else. My heart wasn't in it, and it was clear that my classmates could tell.

But then, what's a girl to do when she goes from the carefree life and stylish clothes of an undergraduate to the harsh realities of waking up before the sun, slinging her hair back in a grimy ponytail, slapping on some chicken-shitty coveralls, and trudging out to her Jeep in positively *enormous* boots? There's only one thing to do: grin and bear it.

Or fall asleep in class. One day, not too long into the semester, I was so tired in class that I fell asleep at my desk. Now, it's one thing to fall asleep in an undergraduate lecture hall, but no one falls asleep in a master's class. No one except me, anyway. I slept so deeply that day that I actually snored myself awake. The moment I heard that honk-snort wakeup call, my heart skipped, and I shot up in my seat. The professor had stopped talking, and every eye in the class turned on me. I was so disoriented and disheartened that it took a moment to register that this wasn't just some bad dream.

I was beyond embarrassed. But I guess it could've been worse. I could've pulled a Cooper and *farted* myself awake.

That day was a wakeup call in more ways than one. The embarrassment was one thing, but I realized then that I had to start taking this process seriously. My heart was still with the prospect of veterinary school, but in the event that I never made it in, I knew I had to graduate with this master's. Having an advanced degree related to working with animals, after all, is better than not having an advanced degree related to working with animals.

Although I would get used to it to some extent, I was never exactly *comfortable* in clothes covered in chicken scat. I did, however, get better about waking early and making it through the day without embarrassing myself. I passed most of my days visiting one of two different farms, one of them set up with numerous coops housing thousands of chickens, and the other playing host to scores of free-range turkeys, which was a whole different scene. I'd spend my late mornings and early afternoons in classes, learning about a subject I couldn't imagine myself ever using while I dreamed of late fall and filling out vet school applications. Then, every night, Cooper and I would hang out. We'd go on walks, throw some humungous sticks around, tussle a little, and turn in early for that 5:30 alarm.

By September 11th, 2001, I'd gotten myself tucked into a reasonable little routine. Maybe that's why the date in question didn't seem such a monumental one at first. I remember I was picking eggs when one of the other girls came in, looking white as a sheet. She was a year ahead of me, and I'd never known her to be anything but unflappable.

"Did you hear?"

I shrugged. I hadn't heard anything yet that morning, apart from clucking.

"Some plane just ran into the World Trade Center."

Looking back, it's kind of shocking how naïve we were, but in that moment, my first thought was that it had to have been an accident.

"What?" I said. "That's stupid. Who was the idiot flying the plane?"

It wasn't until a few minutes later that our professor came in and made it clear that we'd been well out of the ballpark on our guess about what had happened. He switched on a radio, and we picked eggs while we listened to the terror unfold. When the second plane hit, we were all so devastated that none of us was even moving, let alone doing our jobs.

They wound up shutting down Virginia Tech for a few days, as I know they did many schools across the country. Classes were canceled, and we were all left with the harrowing realization that we weren't as safe as we'd been raised to believe. I spent most of those days getting in quality time with Cooper. He had no idea what was going on—how the country seemed to be tearing apart at the seams and then piecing itself back together on the back of a wave of mournful patriotism—and that's exactly why he was such a spectacular companion. He always knew just what to say, which was precisely nothing with his mouth and everything with his eyes.

"All will be well again," he kept telling me with his stare.

And in the end, he was right.

• • •

When I was an undergraduate, the house I shared with my roommates often helped to scratch that city itch I've always carried around with me. There, I could bask in the thrum of urban noise and right myself for the next day. This new place I shared with Hannah didn't afford me the same opportunities. It was down an old country road that ran behind the poultry farms just off campus. The place was the definition of rustic, tucked away in a thicket of trees and surrounded by rolling Virginia farmland. Occasionally we'd catch close sight of an airplane, as the house was situated near a tiny airport where, as fate would have it, I would one day take up a hobby of learning how to fly.

Constructed of dingy brown stone, Hannah's house was a bit on the shabby side. It was the definition of cozy. You'd walk through the door and find a wood-burning stove right there to greet your knees with either a good, metallic clunk or searing hot heat. Just beside it, Hannah kept a sofa. This house didn't believe in entryways, foyers, mudrooms, lobbies, thresholds, anterooms, or ingresses of any kind. When you opened the door, it was just straight living space. Just past the stove and to the left was my bedroom. Straight on past the tiny living room was the kitchen, and attached to that was Hannah's room. Weird setup. The whole affair occupied a single floor featuring decidedly grandmotherly furnishing and décor. It wasn't the roomiest of places, and finding anything to do required a decent drive, but it was peaceful, so it suited us just fine.

The only reason I even bring up the size and locale of the place I occupied with Hannah is because it wouldn't take us long to learn that, while two people can share tight quarters, the effort's a little tougher for two dogs.

For Cooper, at least early on, the move was an upgrade. He still had to sleep and eat in my bedroom, and he still had to hang out in his crate while I was away, but now he had that wide, flat, couple-acre back yard to run and flop around in. On our walks, he could just fly wherever his heart took him. And for the times when I couldn't join him outside, I'd set up a stake for him with a long chain. When it came to that puppy, one thing was for certain: he loved lying for hours in a sunny spot of grass. Whenever I would stress about how much I missed my friends or my old place, or about what was happening in what everyone was suddenly referring to as a "post-9/11 world," I would just watch how Cooper handled it all. Mostly it involved soaking up rays with his tongue hanging out. He wasn't troubled about any of it. He was cool with anything that came his way.

Even though I think he missed his dog friends from the old place, he tried to make do by striking up a friendship with Hannah's dog Penny. Trouble was that Penny wasn't so much into playing. As an old, kind of cranky Cocker Spaniel, she just didn't have the lunatic puppy strength required to keep up with Cooper. This made for some slight tension between Hannah and me at first. We remained friendly, but the fact that our dogs didn't mesh made living together a little like the worst season of Real World you could possibly imagine—something like "Real World Farmland," or maybe "Real World Tiny Cottage." The four of us would've made for compelling cast members in the sense that our personalities resided on different poles. Hannah was right at home on the farm. She was tall and lanky with straight red hair and freckles. She was soft spoken and a little shy. She was a vet student and a stay-at-home-and-study kind of person. These are all fine qualities, but I was exactly none of those things. We still got along well—right up until Cooper started slowly wearing out our welcome.

It took him about six months, but the final straw came down when we had a dog-friend over for him. Kym had moved on to North Carolina State by then, but she would still come up for visits from time to time, and would always bring her Mastiff puppy Cyrus. I'd like to say that it was the bigger of the two dogs that instigated this mess, but the truth was, the spaz award belonged to Cooper. Call it a playdate gone wrong. Or call it two bulls in the constrained china shop that was Hannah's little cottage. Either way, they started off with the typical puppyish roughhousing and chasing before the crazy-train derailed in Cooper's head and nuttiness ensued. Just two young dogs having fun. Being puppies.

Crashing headlong into the TV stand.

For me, it happened in slow motion. I saw every aspect of Cooper's playfully raised fur, every glint in the saliva flying in all directions around the scrabbling dogs. The TV began to teeter at first, then slowly toppled forward. When I called out "Noooo," I heard my own voice deliver in a deep baritone that didn't fit me. For an instant, I thought maybe the TV would survive the fall. It was the most expensive thing in the house, after all, and to my naïve, early-twenties mind, expensive things were supposed to be tougher.

The way it shattered was fantastic and horrifying to see all at once. Cooper and Cyrus looked like synchronized swimmers the way they back-jumped all swan-like away from the TV's splashdown. Then they just kind of stared at it for a second before getting back to what they were doing beforehand. Didn't even faze them. I was so stunned, I'd forgotten how to speak, let alone how to discipline a dog in this kind of scenario. It's not like there's a page in the dog training book for TV destruction anyway. This kind of skill wouldn't win him any dog shows.

All the while, I was thinking, *Oh my God, Hannah's going to kill me.* "Cooper," I seethed. But then when I looked at him, all oblivious to the destruction and having the time of his life as he play-squabbled with his friend, I couldn't bear to hold my anger. He was a dog, and he was merely doing what dogs do. I found it hard to stifle the urge to laugh.

In such a situation, what dogs do is this: they provide their person with the impetus to leave a slowly decaying living situation. Cooper and I could've stuck this one out—could've weathered the entirely righteous storm of passive-aggressive frustration I'm sure we'd have received from Hannah over the remaining six months of my lease—but the future now seemed as crystal clear as the glass lying in a thousand triangular shards all over the hardwood. This was the end of our time on Real World Tiny Cottage.

It was my idea to leave. Hannah was gracious, but there was just too much tension. I was grateful for the opportunity she had given me, but it was clear our lives just didn't mesh. As it turned out, Amy happened to be moving back to Virginia Tech at the time, so my transition worked out perfectly. From this new setting, Cooper and I could start over with clearer heads and calmer hearts. Finally it seemed we'd be able to settle into a normal life.

CHAPTER THREE

Attack, Cooper! Attack!

Our first foray into dog-show culture happened in early August of 2001, at the James River Kennel Club in Lynchburg, Virginia. Given that its central purpose was to host shows just like this one, the building had all the charm of an airplane hangar. The floor looked like dingy green clay tennis courts crisscrossed by accordion fencing. There were bleachers set up for viewing on one side of the cavernous room, but generally the only spectators were the other participants in the dog shows. These affairs were very much by the people and for the people.

Generally the place buzzed with purposeful activity. An outsider unaware of the concept of dog shows might wander in and assume the whole building was full of people trying to keep their chins up as they led their prancing pets around. Everywhere you looked, you'd see a stony-faced talent judge in an alarmingly formal red dress or white jacket. You could throw a rawhide bone in any direction and hit someone currently in the act of fretting over their dog's comb and primp job. I was the youngest participant by at least a decade, and as a fashionable twenty-something just wanting to try something new with my pretty puppy, found myself slightly out of place amid the frump.

The way participants in a dog show obsess about their dog's breed is kind of humorous in part because, to meet them, you would swear that they were their own unique breed of people. And I mean that in the most flattering of ways. They're strange, yes, but they're also undeniably good human beings. They're kind, and most will go out of their way to help you when you're confused. Since I found myself confused at dog shows most of the time, it was nice to have the guiding hands.

Many dog-show people force themselves into little cliques based on their dog's specific breed, but all of them share an uncommon love for animals. It takes a different kind of heart and head to drive up in an Astro van flanked by airbrushed pictures of a Collie or bedecked with bumper stickers that read things like "I love my Pomeranian" and "Caution, Show Dogs." They'd roll up in sweatshirts and trucker hats pressed with giant pictures of their own dog's face, belt buckles formed into metallic silhouettes of their breed of choice, and shoes that put comfort and pace miles before fashion.

The affair in Lynchburg was an all-breed show, which meant that all breeds were welcome to enroll. This made the event quite a bit less formal and rigid than something like Westminster, but that didn't scare away the folks most obsessed about their animals. There were hundreds of them, their dogs all prim and proper and stunningly beautiful. Since I had the kind of dog who obliterated television sets, I figured we didn't stand a chance. He was pretty, sure—and he had the fancy dog-show name of "Taragwyn's King Cooper"—but would his training stand up to the rigor?

"I don't know, Coop," I told him. "Just try to remember to stack." "Stacking" is what show-dog people call it when a dog stands with his head straight up in a still, perfect stance, his tail up and leaning forward so it's perfectly in line with his legs. That's the bread and butter of a champion show dog. That's the thing the judges are looking for above anything else. And it's every bit as crazy as it sounds.

Cooper seemed to understand. He stacked like the king part of his flashy fake name.

My paperwork pointed us to a roped enclosure assigned a number and letter combination that situated us somewhere near the outskirts of the hangar. Here, Cooper and I would participate in a competition against other dogs and people dedicated to the hound group. We'd all vie for the coveted "Best of Breed" before taking our talents into the main arena to reach for that elusive "Best in Show." Along the way, there would be a lot of trotting and turning, teeth-checking and testicle-touching. Cooper had the teeth and the testicles, but I feared the trotting and turning might fall a bit short. He was a good boy, but I wasn't yet sure if he was truly a show dog.

"You ready?" I asked him when it was our turn to run the pen.

I swear he nodded in reply. He looked excited. *Confident,* even. It was almost as if he'd been made just for this kind of occasion. I suppose that's because he was made for just this kind of occasion. For a dog to be considered what people in dog show and breeding circles refer to as a champion, he or she has to win at least thirteen dog shows. As one might imagine, that's tough to do. But *both* of Cooper's parents were champions. He might not have wound up in a home with the kind of person who lives and breathes dog shows, Astro-van style, but he certainly had the genetic predisposition.

That didn't make me any less weirdly nervous. I'd already found that this competition would be friendly, but fierce. I'd been helped out along the way by a number of people, but when Cooper's turn came, I could sense that these same people would be silently hoping that one of us would trip and fall on our face. Not a soul in the room made any bones about whether they were there to win. Victory was the essential magnetism of the event.

Because dog-show people are so kind, our perfect run through the pen made us no true enemies—just opponents who were somewhat less than allies. Cooper and I were already card-carrying members of the English Foxhound Club of America, so we had familiar faces and even friends there with us. I tried to focus on them as I trotted alongside my beautiful dog. These friends had helped me learn the ropes quickly as I tried not to look so much like a college student pretending to be a show person amid the real thing. As I tried to find their faces among the crowd, I saw only intensity staring back at me. That's when I decided to stop worrying about the other people and start worrying only about the potential champion next to me.

Fortunately, despite my best efforts to look as awkward as I felt, Taragwyn's King Cooper's sublime beauty was all we really needed. I might not have had quite enough training at leading him, but his naturally gorgeous, undeniably show-doggy gait made up for any of my shortcomings as a trainer. He won "Best of Breed" that day, and it wouldn't be his last victory either. That's how I began my life as friend to the perfect dog with the paperwork to prove it.

• • •

By then, we'd settled into our new home with Amy, and there, my perfect dog got back to the business of demonstrating just how loose a term "perfect" is when describing a playful puppy. In Cooper's case, the shortfalls in perfection often had to do with some of his more fringe comforts and conveniences. Anyone who has ever had a dog will attest to the notion that finding them exactly the *right* comforts and conveniences can often be a challenge. One can spend twenty dollars on a toy that looks right up the dog's alley but then get it home to be utterly ignored.

In my case, I'd been so excited about him in the lead-up to our first days together that I'd essentially bought out the entire local pet store in my efforts to ensure that he would be as comfortable and happy as possible in his new home. I learned quickly that more than half of the stuff I would never use because it either wasn't necessary or Cooper didn't care for it. We had fancy dog bowls, various leashes, and toys of all sorts and sizes. Out of all of that stuff, though, Cooper's one true nemesis was the brush. I still laugh to think about a show dog so deathly afraid of a brush, but that's exactly what Cooper was. His fear of that harmless utensil was nothing short of abject. I'd learned this on the very first day I brought Cooper home, but it had been quite a while since I tried brushing him, so I figured now that we were in this new, positive environment with Amy, we could give it another try.

The moment I flashed the brush, he bolted from me, tearing around the room in that defensive, ready-to-pounce posture a dog takes on when either fleeing or playing. At first, I didn't realize how terrified he was. It looked like he was having fun, after all. So I tried making a little game out of it.

"I'm gonna get you, Cooper," I said, all sing-songy.

He skittered over the linoleum to the other side of the kitchen. I crouched in a playful stance and approached, brush in hand.

"I'm gonna get you," I repeated, more nasally this time.

He sprang from his corner, nearly knocking me over as he careened between my legs and found my bedroom.

I laughed. "You think you can hide from the brush in there?"

Slowly I crept toward the open door, my smile so huge it hurt. "C'mon, Coop. We've got to brush you eventually."

There I saw him standing tall on the bed. There he saw me, still holding the brush. The moment his eyes met that fearsome object, he tumbled into a squat and held there as if threatening to pee.

"Cooper, don't you dare."

To my great surprise, he listened. He straightened up and looked at me, giving a contented little lick of his chops.

"That's fair. I'll put the brush away as long as you promise not to pee on my bed."

As if agreeing to the deal, he shook his head. I laughed. But then he straight up peed on the bed.

"Oh my God, Cooper!" I screeched as he doused the place where I slept.

When finally it was over, he lowered his head and sat, looking pleased and relieved and entirely oblivious to the mess he'd made. I'd have been mad if the whole thing wasn't so frustratingly funny. It's my opinion that a woman never truly realizes the sheer depth of her capability to love until she has to wash her dog's piss off her comforter and pillow.

Apart from the foibles with piss and brushes, Cooper was a spectacularly good sport in an apartment occupied by two fun-loving young women. Young and fun loving as we were, we still subjected our animals to the usual college-chick-shtick. For instance, we would dress Cooper up in our clothes. Some of my favorite pictures of him are those that feature him all dopey-eyed with one of my hoodies hanging off him.

The whole experience living with Amy was positive. The apartment was warmer and more energetic than the cottage I'd left. My new roommate enjoyed speaking to me and interacting with Cooper. Everything about Amy was comfortable and sweet and light and airy, and everything about our apartment was modern and new and upscale. "Corkie the Yorkie" had gone back to live with Amy's dad, so that removed all tension between Cooper and another dog as well.

This didn't mean that Cooper didn't have any dog friends to play with—quite the contrary. A white German Shepherd named Adia lived on the top floor of the building, and she and Cooper would walk together, play together, and romp around on the tennis courts just outside my ground-floor apartment together. That was the best feature of this new place, in many ways. Whenever Cooper needed to bounce out some energy, I could just grab a tennis ball and throw it onto the courts, where he could chase after the thing to his heart's content.

Of course, all this newfound positivity was helped by the fact that Amy and I shared such a long history. The computers that assigned living spaces for incoming freshmen at Virginia Tech happened to place us in the same corner of our first dorm. In that corner, there were only two rooms, which kind of isolated the two of us and our roommates from the rest of the girls on the floor.

Amy was a striking beauty with long, thick brown hair and long, thin legs. We spoke mostly of heartbreak in the early going, as Amy's mom had passed away a mere three weeks before Amy left for college. The two of us shared remarkably similar backgrounds, but in some ways, it was her personal tragedy that led the two of us to the tight bond we would quickly form and maintain for all these years after.

So there we were living together for the second time, and not much had changed about either of us. This allowed us to settle into a familiar routine with a welcome rapport. Amy had returned to Blacksburg in part because her entry level job hadn't fit her well and in part because of her boyfriend, Robbie, who worked with me at Texas Steakhouse at the time.

Robbie was a jolly guy with a stockier build and red hair that added flavor to his easy sense of humor. He was a fantastic guy to work with, always adding a light touch and making it more fun for me to work a side job I probably didn't have time for but needed in order to make ends meet. Of course, the tips helped—especially on football weekends—and my friends always liked the perk of being able to come into the restaurant and pretend it was their birthdays so they'd get this free, enormous dessert. It was all just part of my new day-in-the-life: go to school in the morning, hit the farm or the lab, spend my free time between classes with Cooper and his tennis court, and work nights at the steakhouse. Most nights, I'd be so tired as to be glassy-eyed and even clumsier than I am naturally. One such night, I dropped a whole tray of drinks on one of my tables. That's embarrassing enough as it is, but that particular table happened to be passing the time by looking at a giant stack of photographs when I assaulted them with various boozes. I'm not sure there was a single picture that made it through un-destroyed.

Fortunately, as poor as I was at waiting tables, I hadn't decided to make a career of it. I kept myself distracted from my food service foibles by cramming as much daydreaming about my future as I could into my busy life. When I was returning steaks that weren't cooked properly, I'd be thinking about my second round of vet school applications. When I was mucking out a filthy chicken coop, I'd be imagining myself receiving an acceptance letter to the vet school at Penn. And whenever my feet ached from a long day of chicken feeding and steak serving, I'd distract myself by pondering my lifelong dream to help an adorable kitten overcome an ear infection with my vet school diploma hanging on the wall behind me.

Not everyone shared my enthusiasm. In fact, there were some who doubted I would ever be able to take that next step. My spirits weren't helped by the fact that the highest profile of these people was my student advisor for my master's program.

His name was Dr. Webber, which felt apt on the day he told me flatly that I would never get into vet school. The way he said it made me feel hopelessly trapped, the spider of my disappointment bearing down on me.

"I'm just not seeing the grades," he said as I tried not to tear up.

Dr. Webber was a round and stout professor with gray hair and kind but unflinching eyes. He was a nice man and a good advisor, but I couldn't help but choke on the advice he was trying to give me that day.

"But I have all this experience," I said, pointing to the relevant lines on my resumé and application. "You told me yourself that experience matters."

He sighed and leaned back in his chair. "I don't like telling you this, Katti. Believe me. This is one of the hardest things I have to do. Your relevant experience is extensive, and your GRE scores are good. But the grades still matter. I just don't see you getting into a school like Penn."

For a heartbeat, my hopes rose. If he meant that I just didn't have the grades for the University of Pennsylvania, that was fine. Penn might have been my dream school, but it was also the top vet school in the country. Not getting in there would be no big loss. It'd be like getting rejected by Harvard or Yale. There were still all these other fantastic institutions that might take me. "So you're just saying that I won't get into Penn."

"No," he said without mercy. "I'm saying that you aren't likely to get into any vet schools with grades like these."

"Since when was a three-five a bad GPA?"

"Places like Penn and Virginia Tech are looking for a perfect four point. There are just too many people who want to be vets and not enough schools to take them. I'm sorry, Katti, but I think you should start planning to move on to something else."

I paused for a moment before the waterworks began. I thought maybe this guy was just putting me on—or maybe revealing a dislike for me after six months of pretending to be my benevolent advisor. I'd had him as a professor in my animal science nutrition class the previous semester, after all, and I hadn't exactly been riveted throughout. It was one of those 8am numbers with so much lecturing and subsequent studying that no amount of coffee could possibly keep a girl alert for every second of the monotony. Maybe he just didn't like me.

"But—" My lips began to quiver, and the tears spilled over my cheeks.

Dr. Webber rocked forward and set his elbows on his desk, that old kindly glint returning to his eyes. "Look, I'm not trying to kill a dream here. I just don't want you to get your hopes up too high. We have to be real about this situation. Getting into vet school isn't easy. It's not for everyone."

"What about the distant schools? UC Davis in California and Ross University in St. Kitts?" It had been Dr. Webber who had first suggested that I might improve my odds if I expanded my search a little. Schools like these are highly exclusive, so they always seek to look somewhat artificially diverse in terms of their students' home zip codes. A school like Penn would prefer to take someone from a distant state like Florida or Washington before they would take a girl who grew up a mere six hours away by car. The reverse, Dr. Webber had told me, would also be true. Because I grew up in Pennsylvania, I could find myself selected to a school like the University of California, Davis over another applicant from Sacramento, even if that applicant had better grades.

"Katti, I'm sorry." Dr. Webber sounded like he really meant it. "You're a great kid. But I think you'd be better served focusing on what you can get out of your master's program."

Silently I cried, but only for a few more seconds. I've always been one to rise to challenges, and to me, this was the challenge of a lifetime. "Well I hear you, Professor. But I don't agree with you." I rose from my chair at his cluttered little desk in his cramped little office overlooking a hefty, view-blocking pine tree on the quad. "I'm getting into vet school. If not on this round, then on the next one. I'm going to keep applying until it happens for me."

"That's certainly your right," he said as I pushed through the door.

Having your dream crushed when you're only twenty-two years old is a difficult thing. It can shatter the spirit. For the next couple of weeks, I enjoyed a constant battle between the dual emotions of doubt and confidence. My lifelong dream had been lifelong for a reason: I always felt I was destined to become a vet. At the same time, Dr. Webber was right: grades are grades. My application strategy had been sounder this time around, and since I'd been through the process once already, I had a better idea of what the country's various vet school deans of admission were looking for in applications, essays, and background. I had applied to all of the most distant schools I could find. Plus, now I was a master's student in a relevant program. But still, grades are black and white. You can fill in all the gray area you want, but you can't escape that black and white.

Fine, I thought during one night of particular anguish. *You can think that if you want to think that, Dr. Webber. But I'm not going to let you get me down. I'm just going to make sure I get into a vet school.*

Cooper chose that moment to hop into bed with me and set his head in my lap.

"You get it, don't you, Cooper?"

He grumbled through a dog sigh. Then he rolled onto his side and jammed his paws into my leg. It was in this way, as happened many nights, that we fell asleep. It was May of 2002—just about exactly a year since I had first suffered the notion that my vet school dream would take some accomplishing.

The next morning, I awoke to a round of letters I'd been waiting on with a bizarre combination of determination and fear. The first was from UC Davis. Hope leaped into my throat for the briefest of moments because the envelope looked thicker than all the rejection letters I had received the previous year. The news was somewhat better in that I had been waitlisted, but I knew enough about how these competitions work to understand that there was no way I would ever get off that list. Essentially this made for the third rejection this round, the letters trickling in since back in April. I'd open another one that morning, too, before turning my attention to the one from Ross University on St. Kitt's. By then, I was feeling so downtrodden that I failed to notice the heft of this envelope. I kept hearing Dr. Webber's voice in my mind, telling me that I would never be a veterinarian.

Now St. Kitt's was, by quite a ways, the most distant program to which I had applied. So on that factor alone, I should have hoped that maybe this letter would bear better news. But there's only so much rejection a girl can take before she starts to anticipate it. My fingers quivered as I pried open the envelope.

Then I read it.

Dear Katti,

Congratulations on your acceptance, and welcome to Ross University School of Veterinary Medicine. In the next few weeks, you will receive a "Preparation for Enrollment" document that contains important information about the next steps in the matriculation process. You will also receive a formal welcome packet, which will contain more detailed information about preparing for your matriculation, as well as all of the documentation necessary to obtain your St. Kitts Student Visa.

From now until you depart for St. Kitts in August, you can feel free to contact me with any questions that you may have regarding the matriculation process. I have provided some general information for you below so that you can begin your preparations. Please make sure that you contact the necessary personnel in the various departments, as they are here to help you.

Again, welcome to Ross University School of Veterinary Medicine, and I look forward to working with you!

Ecstatic doesn't even begin to describe the depth of my reaction. It was a harrowing, humbling, and yet altogether joyful, inside-out kind of feeling. I felt as if my inner child had leaped from my body and was running laps around the apartment. I was so thoroughly pleased by what I had just read that I hardly understood any of it. I failed to read the signature or gather that this letter had come directly from a man who would be my advisor—and was probably someone I should contact as soon as possible. I glossed over the sheer number of times the letter engaged the word "matriculation," which always struck me as an uncomfortably bathroomy-sounding word. It didn't even really occur to me that not only did this letter mean I would be going to veterinary school after all, but that the school's location meant I would be spending a good portion of my early-to-middle twenties in a tropical paradise as well. None of that mattered because the door to my dream had reopened and I was too busy sprinting through it to even remember how to think, let alone process information.

I was going to vet school.

The screech I let loose was unholy.

"What the hell's going on?" Amy jump-stepped from her bedroom. It was still pretty early in the morning, so I'm not sure whether I woke her or just startled her as she tended her morning routine.

I waved the letter over my head as I did that same little dance you do on "The Price is Right" when you win a car.

"You got in!" Amy bellowed.

"I got in!"

She ran to me and we hugged and jumped and hugged. Cooper cocked his head to one side. Then he tried shoving his nose between us as if wanting to join the embrace.

"I did it, Cooper!" I knelt down to nuzzle him, the letter still fluttering in my hand.

Cooper harrumphed.

"Here, let me take a picture." Amy ran to get her camera. When she returned, I was still sidled up with Cooper, my arm slung over his proud shoulders. She gave me a look as if she expected me to get up so we could take a formal picture.

"No, this is perfect," I said. "I want Cooper to be in it." So there I was, grinning up at the camera, my vet school acceptance letter stretched out between my two hands, and Cooper's big, beautiful mug looking out from between my arms.

Later that afternoon, as I was on my way to the steakhouse, I happened to notice the time and realized that Dr. Webber had his office hours right then. So I decided to take a quick stop at his office to rub it in a little. When I knocked, he looked intrigued, and maybe even a little apologetic. I could sense that he hadn't felt good about the way our last meeting had ended. That made showing him the letter even more of a triumph.

"Just wanted you to see this," I said, somewhat taunting but still toeing the line of respectful.

When he took the letter, his eyes widened. "Katti, I—" he said, trailing off. "Katti, this is wonderful. Congratulations."

With a satisfied smirk, I took the letter back, thanked him for his help, and bailed from that office forever. I had faced more than my share of doubt, but now I had gotten into veterinary school.

• • •

The path to my dreams was filled with affordable steak dinners. My employee discount at the steakhouse ensured that I dined on steak and shrimp most nights despite being poor. I'd have to eat really late, since we could only order food for ourselves after our shifts were over, and I'd always have to eat at the bar, but it did make for a nice, casual dining setting most nights. Robbie and I often worked the same shifts, which lined me up for plenty of laughs, and also a carpool opportunity with Amy, who would invariably want to take advantage of any chance to come see her boyfriend for a bit while he finished cleaning up after his shift.

It was on one of those occasions—dining on steak with Robbie while we waited for Amy to come pick me up—that I received the call that would bring the winged unicorn of vet-school-pride I was riding to an abrupt, lurching stop. I was tucked away in the left corner of the bar, right near the door. My little huddle of diners included Robbie, the bartender, and our manager, Reese. When my pre-2000s brick of a cellphone rang, I answered quickly, expecting a call from Amy telling me that she had arrived.

By the time I pressed the phone to my head, I could already hear the hollering from the other end of the line. My company gave me those glassy-eyed stares of concern.

"Attack!" Amy was screaming through tears. "Attack, Cooper! Attack!"

I froze, every muscle tightening. A chilling tingle of fear gripped me from within. "What are you saying? Amy, did Cooper attack you?"

She was frantic. I could hear a struggle in the background. "Attack…" she kept murmuring between sobs. "Cooper… Attack… Cooper attack." And then she hung up.

Panic washed over me. All I could picture was Amy with bite wounds everywhere, blood flying as she struggled to get Cooper off her. The pit in my stomach was boring right through me. I couldn't stop shaking.

"Robbie, can I get a ride back to my place?" The tears welled up in my eyes.

"Of course. What's going on?"

"I'll explain in the car."

Obviously, there wasn't much to explain. That only made Robbie drive faster. What we didn't know at the time was that Amy's call had come from her car, and that Amy was already heading to the steakhouse. So we passed each other in opposite directions somewhere along Highway 460.

When we arrived at the house, we both shot out of Robbie's car and keyed our way through the door.

"Amy?"

"Amy, where are you?"

The house was empty. Dark. I found myself flicking on every light, searching for signs that my dog had mauled my friend. My heart was pounding. Room after room, I found nothing. No sign of a struggle. No blood anywhere. Now my panic gave way to confusion. I called Amy's phone. She didn't answer.

"What do we do?"

"I don't know," Robbie said.

"Should we check with the hospital?"

"We could call them, I guess, but they probably wouldn't tell us even if she *has* checked in already."

"So we just wait?"

He raised his hands. "I don't know what else we *can* do."

Just as he finished the thought, we heard the key in the front door. We rushed over, dripping with anxiety. When the door swung open, Amy walked in, shaken but clearly unbitten. She was white as a sheet, and her keys were jangling in her hand.

"Amy, what's going on?" Robbie asked.

"Are you okay?" I said at the same time.

Then, in bounded Cooper, looking as right as the day is long. His tail was wagging and his tongue hanging out. He plowed into my legs, just like he always did, nuzzling up and accepting my patting hands.

"Did he… Did Cooper *attack* you?"

Amy let out a sigh. "He didn't attack me," she said softly. "He had an attack."

"An attack? What do you mean?"

By now, Robbie was ushering Amy over to the couch. They sat with his arm slung over her shoulders as she explained herself. Meanwhile, Cooper sidled up to me, panting happily as I caressed his head.

"We were in the car on our way to pick you up." Robbie's embrace seemed to calm Amy, so the words came easier now. "I heard this noise in the backseat, and when I looked in the mirror, it was like his eyes had rolled back in his head. He just fell over and started shaking. I called out to him, then started screaming for him, but he wasn't responding. He was just lying there between the seats."

At the time, I was unexperienced in matters like these, so I found myself not entirely believing Amy's account. Besides, I knew that Cooper was in perfect health, both every day I had known him and right now as he sat beside me. Even as we spoke, he got up and show-trotted to his water bowl to have a big, slurpy drink. There was nothing about him that seemed anything but completely normal.

That night, I watched him closely to make sure all was well, but the more I witnessed, the more I questioned whether Amy's account was entirely accurate. It was part ignorance and part willful need to disbelieve the idea that Cooper could be severely and terrifyingly ill, but by the end of the night, all my stresses on the matter had evaporated. *Cooper must've just had an especially spastic moment,* I thought.

Little did I know that the first attack of my dog's life was like opening a Pandora's box.

CHAPTER FOUR

Litters and Lines

The next morning, I had to rush off to my manual labor at the chicken farm, which meant that Amy would have to be alone with Cooper again. Well, not alone. Robbie had stayed over, and he promised to be the calming hand.

As I headed out, I tried not to worry about Cooper. I had already convinced myself that, even if what Amy had seen had been an actual attack of some kind, it was just a bump in the road. Besides, if there was something wrong, I could just take him to one of the capable vets at VT and they would fix him right up. That's what vets do, after all. That's why I was going to become one.

My path to that dream boasted a fish-out-of-water sort of charm. Picture me as a city girl standing in the center of a circle of onlookers on a chicken farm. The onlookers consist of a couple of professors, some farm staff, and the one other master's student on farm detail with me that morning, a bright-eyed good friend named Christa. Like Christa and everyone else present, I'm standing there in coveralls and boots caked in bird shit. The two of us had spent much of the morning hauling around sacks of feed, making sure the chickens were healthy, adjusting their diets, and entering all the information into our charts. Now it was time for us to learn the invaluable lesson of how to execute a sick chicken. This wouldn't be the most essential lesson for a future vet to know, but I still had to get through this semester in good standing or I'd find my acceptance to St. Kitt's under reconsideration.

It turns out that to kill a chicken in what is apparently considered the most humane way possible, you have to wring its neck with some sudden and serious centrifugal force. The way you do this is to pick the chicken up by the head and sort of fast-pitch softball it until it, like, succumbs to natural causes. If this sounds like a horrifying, albeit alarmingly simple process, that's because it is.

My professor, ever the one to delight in my city-girl squeamishness, chose me as the lucky contestant to demonstrate the art before the gathering. Now I've never been a stellar athlete, but I'd thrown a softball before, so I had a pretty good idea of the kind of speed and force I'd have to work up to get the job done. What no one told me is that you don't let the chicken go at the typical softball release point.

With all eyes on me, I gathered up my poor, sick chicken, took a deep breath, wound her in a perfect arc, and then launched her clear across the room. Everyone watching me broke into that noise that says they're part horrified and part so amused that they can hardly contain themselves. It was a sad sight, that dying chicken rocketing into the far wall. But give the old girl credit: she got right back up, shook it off, and waddled away as if it was just another day at the office.

"Did that just happen?" Christa said, awestruck.

That's when everyone just died laughing.

It's hard to imagine a scenario where I would've been happier to hear my phone ring. But the truth was that all morning, I'd been dreading the idea that it could ring at any second with news I didn't want to receive. When I saw the familiar number on the caller ID, my heart sank.

Amy was right about Cooper all along.

• • •

It didn't take me long to size up the scene when I returned home. Cooper seemed unusually tired. Amy had gone sheet-white again, and Robbie was explaining how they had heard a ruckus from Cooper's crate, and had found him lying down, foam on the side of his mouth, his water bowl overturned and water pooling everywhere.

"So you didn't see him seize?"

"No, but he was acting really weird afterward," Robbie said. "We let him out of his crate and he just kind of paced around all dazed and confused."

"And his eyes were really glassy for a while," Amy added. "He just kept circling and circling like he had no idea what he was doing."

I should have believed my roommate by that point, but the truth was, I just couldn't accept the possibility that this was actually happening. In my head, I kept telling myself, *I don't know what they think they saw, but there's no way my dog was seizing.* Cooper was just too young and too healthy—and too expensively purebred and beautiful besides—for him to have such a significant genetic defect. He was a *show dog*, after all. How could he possibly be falling apart like this? There had to be some mistake.

My attempts to rationalize the situation would fall apart soon enough. An hour later, Cooper had his third seizure, and I experienced a height of panic I had never seen before. It was around 11am. Amy and Robbie had left. I was tending to some busy work in the living room when suddenly my dog made the strangest sound. I turned just in time to see him jump up and start running forward, his head turned backward, and this look on his face as if he had seen a ghost. He plowed into the Jack and Jill bathroom attached to my bedroom. There, he fell right in front of the bathtub and rolled into a full-blown, violent seizure. He was shaking, his mouth open and frothing. It lasted for twenty seconds but felt more like six hours. I was so tense as I watched that, the moment it ended, I felt like collapsing myself.

"Cooper!" I kept screaming. "Cooper, are you okay? Cooper!"

When it was over, I knelt down to comfort him. He blinked through his confusion and rose up enough to lay his head on my lap. For a few minutes, he couldn't have been more docile. I could practically feel his fear as I passed my hand slowly over his forehead again and again.

The fog of my own hysteria was thick, but my first instinct remained sound. It was to call Christa, the friend

I figured was in the best position to offer me good advice and a helping hand.

"Help!" I yelled into the phone. I was screaming and crying like a madwoman.

"Katti, calm down," Christa said. "Just tell me what's happening."

I began shuddering through my waning sobs. "Cooper had a seizure. I need help."

Christa and her kindhearted husband Kevin were at my apartment within minutes. The way they managed to calm me and help me get Cooper ready to visit the vet was nothing short of amazing. It wasn't my finest hour in the sanity department, but they helped me keep it all together.

We loaded Cooper into the car and took him to the vet, whose office was near campus, maybe a five-minute drive from where Amy and I lived. Cooper had been here a few times before, but always for routine checkups and innocuous things like puppy shots. Now I was bracing to learn whether my dear friend had a serious condition that would affect his life forever.

After some tests and some questioning, Cooper and I set up for an impossibly long wait to learn the results. I passed the time thinking darkly about how this was exactly the kind of place I longed to work one day. I didn't like the idea that I would one day have to tell a devoted pet lover like me that their pet was seriously ill, but at the same time, my desire to help trumped it all.

When the vet finally returned, I learned that I had an epileptic dog. Even though I had seen evidence of it with my own eyes, this was difficult news to accept. Cooper was a puppy. The picture of health. It didn't make sense. But now he'd be on a phenobarbital prescription and I'd be under strict orders to watch his behaviors and moods.

Even as we drove home with a bottle full of weirdly small barbiturates, I was still telling myself not to believe it entirely. We would learn to manage this somehow. We would deal with it and lead otherwise normal lives together. We'd just set up a pill-popping schedule and everything else would be even keel. And eventually, as long as we stuck to the schedule, Cooper would return to being that happy-go-lucky buddy of mine.

• • •

It's unnerving to be sitting next to a dog who, at least a few times a day, starts quivering uncontrollably. But that's what was happening to Cooper. His standard, epileptic-style seizures started to share time with an equally horrifying occurrence called focal seizures.

Maybe the most unsettling thing about a seizure like this is that there isn't usually any noise that alerts you to the fact it's happening. At least that's how it was with Cooper. We'd just be sitting there together on the couch under the warm glow of the TV or in the grass under the warm glow of the sun, and I'd have this premonition that something was wrong. Then, there he'd be, all tense at the shoulders, his eyes rolling back and forth, his lips moving like Mr. Ed, or his head jerking in quick, violent tweaks. Dead silence while all this is happening. The rest of him would look normal. His gaze would be trancelike. It would just be his head and face and eyes and mouth tremoring.

From a medical or veterinary perspective, it's a startlingly unusual thing to encounter focal seizures and standard seizures happening concurrently, as they tend to be related to two completely different circumstances. That's why Cooper's vet was troubled enough about the whole situation to send us to see a neurologist. A dog having a standard seizure is relatively normal. Dogs present with epilepsy with some frequency. But a focal seizure is a different abnormality entirely. It turns out that they're indicative of much rarer and more bizarre conditions.

So off we packed for Virginia Tech's vet school to see the neurologist. My mom and dad had come up for the weekend to provide moral support and to help me take care of my newly ailing dog. They climbed into the passenger and back seat as I let Cooper hop up through the back hatch.

My mom is a petite five-footer with short blond hair and a superlatively pretty face. She's also blessed with the biggest heart and the sweetest personality you'll ever encounter. On top of that, she's humble, helpful, loving, and ever attentive to my needs, the needs of my two sisters Heidi and Gretchen, and even to my sisters' friends and mine. She's just a really good mom. So there she was, there to help, as always, and volunteering more of her time and effort than she needed to volunteer, as always. She sat in the backseat with Cooper, keeping watch over him.

"Now when we get there, if you want us to come back with you, we'll come back with you."

That was my dad, his brown eyes reassuring as I threw my ride in reverse and backed down the driveway. I've always seen something of my own face reflected in my father's. Many have told me that I look exactly like him. We certainly share the same Germanic features. I like to think my dad's a bit rougher around the edges than I try to be, but in an exceedingly good way. He's a blue-collar kind of guy. He's a tall, stocky, burly plumber by trade. He's the best dad a girl could ask for. A man of few words, certainly, but always sweet and loving, and always one to make sure his daughters are taken care of. Always.

"Just don't be afraid to ask questions," he added.

I gave a soft smile as I rolled us onto the street and started heading for that old familiar building. The place was one of those architectural acts of aggression so common in the 70s—all stark façades, dark arrays of floor-to-ceiling windows, and sandwich-bread layers of squared, rain-darkened concrete. It wasn't the most inviting-looking place, but it was where I would take Cooper in the hopes of curing his alarming potential conditions.

We parked and made our way in through the front door. We found the neurology department and walked my friend down the long, white, sterile hallways with the fluorescent overhead lights, the cinderblock walls, and the rows of plastic chairs lined up here and there on one side.

At the check-in desk, I informed the receptionist of our arrival and the purpose of the visit. She referred us to the nearest set of plastic chairs and let us know that a vet tech would be out to see us shortly. Minutes later, we were following a straight-out-of-college-age vet tech with strawberry blond hair and a long stride into a room like any other veterinary examination space. Cooper's hundred pounds made him too big to hop onto one of those space-age stainless steel exam tables, so the checkup would take place on the floor as I nuzzled his head for comfort. The tech cooed at him and expressed her sorrow that he had to be in here at all.

"Yeah," was all I could manage.

I was nervous now. I'd done a bit of internet research on the subject of focal seizures, and it seemed to me that there weren't many prognoses that were anything better than grim. My only real hope was that maybe the seizures themselves had been misdiagnosed. Maybe Cooper was just a weirdo about everything, *including* his epilepsy. Epilepsy we could live with—for a good, long time. I just didn't want it to be one of those diseases with grave initials.

Eventually, the tech let us know that the neurologist would be in to see us in just a few minutes, then left. My parents and I passed the time with uncomfortable small talk about what a nice vet school this must be if they employ technicians as caring and attentive as the one we'd just met. I might have dwelled on the notion that I still felt a little cheated not to have been admitted here, but the truth was that I was so wrapped up in finding out what was going on with Cooper that the thought didn't really cross my mind. I was curious to see the inner workings of the VT vet school, to be certain, but mostly I was just nervous and scared for my dog.

When the door swung open again, in walked a man wearing a lab coat and a sympathetic gaze. His brown hair was parted to the right, no nonsense, and he shined a soft expression that said he was sorry before he even said he was sorry.

"I'm sorry we have to meet like this," he said. "But I hear we're having some problems with seizures."

I nodded and threw my arm around Cooper, who had come to sit at my side. His tongue was hanging out as he panted in that happy, playful way of his.

"So this must be Cooper," the neurologist said. He was younger than I expected—maybe in his mid-thirties—and his kindness was immediately apparent. But then, so was the fact that he knew we were dealing with something really abnormal in Cooper here. We'd be ordering up some tests, I knew, but I also knew that this veterinarian already believed the prognosis wasn't going to be something anyone wanted to hear.

"When he has these seizures, what kinds of things is he doing?"

My explanation seemed to confirm his suspicion. He was pulling a little penlight from his pocket now. He gently held my dog's snout and slid his thumb up to keep Cooper's right eye open. Then he shined the light in quickly and moved on to the other.

"And can you give me an idea of how often this happens?" he asked as he stared into Cooper's retinas.

"I can." I looked away from Cooper for a moment to signal for my mom to bring over the journal I'd been keeping. It was a typical black-and-white bound notebook, but I had turned it into a detailed ledger of Cooper's daily activities. Whenever he seized, I would enter the date and time, the duration of the seizure, and what the seizure looked like. I would also write down whether there was anything different about Cooper's life on that particular day. I kept records of whether the moon was full, whether he had been under an unusual amount of stress that day, whether anything dramatic had happened to throw him off his usual routine, and so on. I wanted to ensure that I included any detail on anything that might have set him off, and anything that might show a correlation. Call it an overly scientific mind. Call it over-exuberance about starting vet school in the fall. I call it abiding love for a puppy.

When my mom handed me the journal, I flipped it open to the most recent entries and showed it to the neurologist.

"These are records of every event." He sounded impressed.

"There's a pattern emerging. He's having these seizures in clusters. He'll have a bunch of them over a few days, and then doesn't have any for a while." Eventually, I would learn that he had his clusters of seizures every seventeen days on the nose. It never failed. On the seventeenth day after his last seizure, he would begin another cycle. It was almost as if his brain had a reboot schedule.

"That's good," the neurologist said.

"That he's having them in clusters?"

He gave a sympathetic frown. "No, I just meant that it's good you're keeping these kinds of records. The more we know, the better we'll be able to help Cooper."

I could feel my parents step closer. Not for the first time on that weekend, I was glad they were there.

"So how do we help Cooper?" My eyes were starting to water from the fear and anxiety.

As the neurologist explained the course of tests they would have to run on my poor dog that afternoon, I found the litany of information both harrowing and intriguing. As a girl in love with a puppy, to hear that he needs a spinal tap and CT scan is about enough to make the room spin. But at the same time, as a girl who aspires to help puppies in need of spinal taps one day, it's fascinating to hear the procedure described.

I spent the next few minutes waffling on the border between heartbreak and fascination as I learned that Cooper would need to be sedated and then fully anesthetized. The sedation would come via IV fluids delivered by a catheter inserted into Cooper's front leg, down near his wrist. The anesthesia would also be injected into the catheter, and then sustained by gas administered through an endotracheal tube.

"He'll be completely asleep when you do the spinal tap?"

My dad reached out and put his hand on my shoulder.

"He'll have to be," the neurologist said not unkindly. "This particular procedure requires precision. We can't have him moving around."

When he saw that the thought troubled me, he softened his tone further. "It'll be okay, Katti. I've done this hundreds of times. When he wakes up, he won't be any worse for wear. And he won't even know anything happened." He gave a gallows chuckle. "The only difference is that he'll have a silly bald spot on the back of his neck."

"Okay." I nodded through tears.

For the first time, I noticed that he was scratching Cooper's back as he spoke. I don't know why, but that always stuck out to me. It made me understand that he really did care. "When we're done with the spinal tap, the CT scan is easy. He'll still be sedated, but he'll just be lying on a gurney as he goes through the machine. That part's just to take pictures of his brain so we can get a better idea of what's going on."

He took a step back and a deep breath. "Now comes the part I always hate about these consultations," he said, his expression contorting into apology.

I couldn't imagine what would be more hateworthy than explaining invasive testing on a dog's central nervous system, so I braced myself for another blow to the heart. The blow came instead to my wallet.

"The estimate for these two tests tends to be high," he explained. "Depending on how much trouble we have anesthetizing him, they usually run about fifteen hundred dollars altogether."

Holy crap, I thought. *That's a lot of money.*

"That's a lot of money."

Suddenly my dad's hand was on my shoulder again. I could hardly feel it, in all the shock and confusion.

"I understand. There's a down payment required before the procedure, with the rest due when you come back to pick him up."

I nodded. "Okay, that's fine."

"Honey, are you sure you want to do this?" Mom asked.

"That's a lot of money," Dad reminded.

"I know." But I didn't think twice. "I guess that's why I got the credit card."

I pondered how I'd gotten that credit card as I walked numbly back to the front desk to make my down payment, which turned out to be $750—a large sum for me back then, but less than a drop in the bucket when compared to the financial saga to come. I'd gotten the card the day I began my postgraduate career. I'd been one of those naïve twenty-two-year-old suckers who had wandered over to the predatory credit card desk on orientation day. I'd like to say that it was the promise of free swag that got me to sign on the dotted line for a credit card I didn't really know how to handle at that age, but the truth was that it took far less than that. I signed up for that card because it allowed me to choose the image I could have printed on the front. That meant I could have beagle puppies. *Beagle puppies!* Saying no to a credit card I didn't really need? Sure. I could do that. But how could a girl say no to *beagle puppies* printed on a card?

So, with my parents looking on from behind me—probably shaking their heads at how irresponsible this all seemed—I swiped my puppy card. $750 changed hands virtually, but I didn't feel even one ounce lighter, financially speaking. It didn't matter to me how I would pay this back. I just had to do it.

When it was done, I went back to give Cooper a long hug and tell him I loved him. Then my parents petted him and said their goodbyes and good lucks. The tech returned and helped the neurologist lead Cooper into the preparation room. The last I saw of my friend before the procedure, he was trotting toward the operating room and the anesthetic that awaited him—trotting in that show dog way of his, proud and gorgeous as ever.

• • •

"Lysosomal Storage Disease," said the neurologist.

These days, I'm familiar enough with the term to know that it's an incredibly rare hereditary disease that can be devastating. Back then, they were just terrifying words.

Cooper was still back in the kennel, recovering from his afternoon of shaving and poking and prodding and drug-induced sleep. So I stood there feeling far too lonely even with my parents by my side and a genuinely downtrodden veterinary specialist presenting the grave news. We were in the waiting room, which had seemed a small space but now felt sprawling and cavernous, as if I had shrunk to a preschool perspective. I felt three feet tall and completely baffled by the world around me.

"So what does that mean?"

He looked worried that I might explode into tears again. He was correct. "Maybe we should take this in the exam room," he suggested.

So we followed him into the same room where he had first explained the $1,500 procedures that would reveal this terrible Lysosomal thing.

"I'm sorry, Katti. This is a rare condition, and I'm afraid there is no treatment. The best we can do is try to prolong Cooper's life and keep him comfortable for as long as we can."

"And how long can we do that?"

He sighed. "A few months. Maybe a year. I hate to say this, but he isn't likely to live more than another year."

Devastation and despair. That's all I remember about the rest of the time we spent in that vet school. We would have had to wait another hour or so before the anesthetic would've worn off enough for Cooper to travel, but I have no recollection of what happened or what was said.

Somehow, we got back to my apartment. Somehow, my friends had gotten word of the dire news and had managed to assemble for our arrival. Christa and Kevin were there, and of course, Amy and Robbie. I thanked them all for their support. Cooper trundled off to my room to lie down. I cried with my parents. Whenever there was a lull in the conversation about what in the world I was going to do with my poor, sick puppy, I would steal a look at him. He was so peaceful, lying there in his open crate, sleeping off what must have been a terrible post-op hangover. I wanted to hug him and to tell him that everything would be all right, but for the first time since I'd known him, it was clear that everything *wouldn't* be all right. My totally normal, gorgeous, happy-go-lucky, King Cooper of a puppy would be dead in less than a year.

It isn't an easy thought for a pet lover to hold in her head.

It was then that I remembered another pet lover in Cooper's life who might want to know about this. The neurologist had called Lysosomal Storage Disease hereditary, which meant that it could be affecting any number of other dogs in Cooper's familial line. Julie would probably want to know about this.

I checked my watch. It was nearly nine o'clock in the evening—a long day of waiting and suffering and waiting. "Do you think I should call his breeder?"

"Why don't you sleep on it?" my mom suggested. "It's a little late to give someone in her situation this kind of news."

She was right, of course. That didn't change how I felt—how desperately I wanted to call Julie to warn her about Cooper's line. It was about enough to make me crawl out of my own skin. I don't know how long I was at it, but I stopped fretting the moment I felt the cold, wet touch of Cooper's nose against the back of my thigh. I turned to see my friend looking up at me, his big eyes burdened by worry. This is exactly why it is impossible to love anything or anyone in quite the same way you can love a dog: Even though he had just endured the worst day of his life, and even though his life would be over soon, his only concern in the world was for me.

I knelt and held him for a long time.

And then the strangest thing happened. Someone must have slid open the sliding glass door a crack, because a gentle breeze wafted into the room, and with it came the most unexpected sight.

It was a dragonfly—a pretty, shiny blue thing that buzzed gracefully around the kitchen, hovered between Cooper's face and mine, and then disappeared out the door again. Upset as I was, the sight of that beautiful bug brought me calm. I couldn't remember ever seeing a dragonfly anywhere other than near an established body of water, and yet there was no such water anywhere near that apartment. This dragonfly had to have traveled a long way from its home to find us. From the way it flew, it was almost as if it had come to deliver a message. I just couldn't quite put my finger on what that message could be.

"What could it mean?" Christa said.

"I don't know. But, I mean, what was it even *doing* here?"

"It's like it was trying to tell you something," Kevin said.

I looked down at my poor puppy, whose face was pressed to my lap. He looked as docile as I had ever seen him.

"It seemed to calm Cooper, too," I said.

"We should look it up," Amy said.

It's funny to think back to a time when the act of gathering knowledge from the Internet wasn't so ubiquitous, but that's how it was in late 2001. I'm not sure which hilariously outdated search engine I used, but eventually I stumbled upon an article suggesting that dragonflies were good omens. I learned that, in China, the dragonfly is considered one of the most powerfully positive symbols one can encounter. The culture interprets the spirit of a dragonfly as representing prosperity, longevity, and even renewal of life.

"Prosperity," Amy read as she stood over my shoulder and stared down at the article on my laptop. "*Longevity*. That *has* to be a good thing in Cooper's case."

"Renewal of life," I read. Then I broke into a broad, if somewhat forced, smile. "How random was it for a dragonfly to show up today of all days?"

Amy was quick to agree. "Completely. I don't think I've ever seen one in the yard, let alone in the house."

"It must mean that the prognosis is wrong." I furrowed my brow. "Renewal of life," I repeated as I read the article a second time.

A part of me doubted the veracity of a web article about dragonfly spirits, but a much larger part of me wanted desperately to believe it. After several days of watching Cooper battle against unseen ghosts, the notion that a calming spirit had entered our lives just felt too soothing to ignore. Maybe Cooper's situation wasn't so dire after all.

• • •

The next morning, my vision glazed from a sleepless night, I found Julie's number in my journal and dialed it with a shaky hand. I'd started a pot of coffee in the kitchen. The percolator was just starting to spurt and gurgle that alluring aroma into the air as I found a seat on the sofa and waited out the ringtone. I couldn't get the thought out of my head: all those other puppies I had met the day I had chosen Cooper. Would any of them have to suffer as Cooper would suffer? Would any of them die young too? Would any of their owners be as devastated by it all as I was?

I just wanted to make it right. But that was the only thing I couldn't do. So the next best thing was to at least inform.

"Hello?" came the still familiar voice.

"Julie?" I said. I had a quick bout with my eyes watering up, but I sucked it up with a deep, leveling breath.

Julie confirmed that she was indeed Julie. I explained to her who I was as if she might not remember me. She did deal with many, many customers, after all. To her credit, she remembered me well.

"And how is Cooper?"

"I just wanted to call to let you know something about him. He's been having seizures, and since it's hereditary, I thought I would let you know so we can warn all the other puppies' families."

I didn't quite know how to react to the silence. It sounded almost like she was distracted—like there was somewhere else she would rather be at the moment. So I did my best to explain the situation as concisely as possible. When I dropped the words "Lysosomal Storage Disease," I don't know what I was expecting—shock perhaps? What I got instead was a total lack of surprise.

"And how did you find that out?"

"I took him in for a CT scan and spinal tap."

"Huh."

Then more silence. It was so unsettling.

I started to speak. "So, I guess . . ." I didn't know what to say.

"Yeah, I already kind of knew this."

An angry brand of confusion surged through me. "I'm sorry?"

"I was told that something was wrong with the other puppies. And some of the others died."

"Died?"

"They either died of natural causes or their owners had to have them put to sleep."

I could feel my face flush and my hands went so numb I nearly fumbled the phone.

"The other puppies are dead already?"

"Six of them anyway."

She made the statement so casually that I honestly didn't think I had heard her correctly. So I asked her to repeat herself.

"We think maybe one was just kicked by a horse," she said. "Another of them they just found dead one day. There were a couple that were having so many seizures that they just had to put them down."

It's difficult to describe the combination of confusion and rage and sadness storming within me all at the same time. "So six of them died," I said through gritted teeth. "But there were eight. Cooper's one. Who's the other?"

"I'm not really sure what happened to him. He went off to South Africa with his family. So no one's sure what's going on there."

Now it was my turn to fall silent, as the rage was winning the war in my heart. It took a good long while to calm myself enough to speak in a levelheaded way.

"Katti? Are you still there?"

"I'm here," I said, my mind reeling. "I'm just wondering why I'm only just now finding out about this."

Back to silence.

"I mean, it would have been helpful to know that all of my dog's siblings were dead."

"I don't know what to tell you, Katti. I'm sorry that he's sick."

From the way she said it, I could sense she meant that my sick dog wasn't her problem—that the transaction was over, and all sales are final. She wasn't thinking about my dog as my best friend, but as a nonrefundable product she had sold me. I suppose it's easier to think that way when you breed dogs for a living, but it still struck me as a little heartless for someone who surrounds herself with such lovable animals.

Sometimes in movies, when a character is furious, you'll get one of those shots where everything takes on a blood-red hue. Before that moment, I'd used to think that the red-sight bit was just a camera gimmick and that "seeing red" was just an expression. That day on the phone with Julie, I learned that seeing red is a very real thing.

"So I guess . . ." That's how I started out, but the tears welling up in my eyes forced me to stop for a moment and collect myself. "I guess I just wanted to tell you that if all of these dogs are dead or dying, maybe you shouldn't be breeding their parents again."

"Cooper's parents are champions," she said. "Champions. You've seen how beautiful their puppies are. Cooper was one of the prettiest dogs I've ever seen."

My first thought was, *How can she even* think *about putting other families through this?* But then I noticed how she was speaking about Cooper in past tense—and the thought that he had a strong chance of dying like all his siblings made me feel like falling to the floor and curling into a ball. "You shouldn't be breeding them again," I said.

"Well…" she said, trailing off. "I'm going to."

With that, she hung up. And with that, I made up my mind that if I couldn't prevent other unborn puppies from sharing the same fate as Cooper, then I was going to do everything within my power—no matter what it cost me—to help Cooper beat the odds and live a long, happy, high-quality life.

In many ways, this was the day our journey together began.

CHAPTER FIVE

Living Will

My red Jeep Cherokee idled in the parking lot. It was packed to the brim with everything I owned—or at least everything I owned that was worth keeping through the transition home and then on to the sunny beaches and thick textbooks awaiting me in St. Kitts. Three people I loved were making those skittering, last-minute preparations everyone makes whenever someone is engaged in a permanent move. My dad futzed around with the car, trying to pack everything just perfectly so Cooper would have plenty of room in what remained of the backseat. My mom was running through the checklists she and I had brainstormed. Amy was helping me sweep through the apartment in search of anything I might have forgotten to pack. Neither of us was entirely ready for me to leave.

For the second time in just over a year, I faced that bittersweet feeling of transition and loss that can only come from graduating to a new period of one's life. I was intensely excited to begin my training as a veterinarian, but at the same time, I was seeing my time in Blacksburg come to a close. It broke my heart, the thought of having to leave Amy and that life we'd shared in college behind.

Until the very end of this transition, my mind let me cling to unreasonable denial. Somehow, I was able to hold back the emotional toll by telling myself, *Oh, this isn't as permanent as it seems. I'll be back soon. And nothing's really going to change. All my friends will still be my friends. I'm just changing scenery for a while.* Then it hit me that this was one of those turning point moments—one of those times when circumstances arrive to change your life to where it's never the same again.

I think Amy and I both shook off that denial and realized the full gravity of the situation at the same time. We were standing in my empty former bedroom, each of us having combed every corner. Now there was nothing left to search, nothing but our own feelings about what was happening. We gave each other one of those watery stares that happen when you're just standing and waiting for the other person to start crying first.

"Well, at least you'll never have to wash chicken shit out of your clothes again."

I tumbled into laughter, and we into a parting hug goodbye.

"You'll come back to visit, right?"

I promised. "And you'll come visit me in St. Kitts, right?"

She promised.

Even though I was certain that Amy and I were both dedicated enough as friends to never lose touch, we both probably knew that the promises we made that day were empty ones. Amy had her life in Blacksburg. I had vet school some thirteen hours away by jet plane. The miracle that was AOL Instant Messenger would allow us to keep in touch, but it would be a long time before we would see each other again.

"I'll IM you when I get settled in," I told her.

She nodded through her tears.

I didn't cry until the moment when I hopped into the driver's seat and we started honking and waving goodbye to Amy. Cooper was there in the backseat, panting happily even though he was so surrounded by the pieces of my life that he couldn't possibly even see out the window to know what was going on.

The drive home was a long one. I followed my dad over the hilly, picturesque Highway 19 through the greenery of the Appalachians. Then it was on to Interstate 79 and the childhood home that awaited at the end of a six-hour haul of everything I owned in the world. Every so often, Cooper's gas threatened to melt the enamel off the dashboard, but every time I whined at him about it, I would take a look in the rearview, get an eyeful of his smiling mug, and laugh it all away. Cooper always knew just how to take a girl's mind off the heavy things.

It was early August, and now we faced less than a month to prepare me to move to an entirely different country in pursuit of a dream I'd held since I was seven years old. I spent much of the time rushing around in a manic sort of way, then crashing hard every night and sleeping the glorious sleep only experienced by people who are either younger than thirty or dead. My heart was constantly aflutter about what awaited me at the end of the month, but at the same time, I carried around guilt and regret and confusion about what I was going to do with Cooper. My parents and I kept talking about how a dog with his kind of condition wouldn't make it any easier for me to study in that first semester, but it still wasn't easy for any of us to think about leaving him with my parents. I didn't want to part with my best friend. And for my parents, I'm pretty sure the thought of taking on a dog whose care needed to be so precise was a pretty stressful one.

Then Cooper started seizing again. It was the seventeenth day on the nose since his last bout. This one was particularly bad. Just before it started, I had almost convinced myself that I could manage everything—a move abroad, an adjustment to a vastly different life and culture, assimilating to a new collection of friends and acquaintances, figuring out how not to fail at vet school, and taking care of a dog with an exotic medical condition and pill-heavy care regimen at the same time. Cooper's latest round of seizures was a wakeup call for me. I wanted to be a supermom dog owner, but my life wasn't going to allow it.

"I don't think I can take him with me," I told my parents. "At least not for the first semester."

They nodded gravely. I could see that they knew this was the right decision for me, but at the same time, now they had to assume responsibility for a seizure-afflicted dog I loved dearly.

"It's just for a while. Just this semester. I'm going to get myself settled in, figure out how to do this vet school thing, and then maybe he can come join me for the second semester."

"Whatever makes sense," my dad said.

"We'll see how it goes," Mom added a little more doubtfully. I think she felt this would be a transition moment for them, as well—one of those situations where everyone's telling themselves that something permanent is in fact temporary. She had been there for Cooper's diagnosis, after all. My guess is that she and my dad had already prepared themselves to be the ones that would have to bury my dog.

I was determined not to let that happen. Every time Cooper seized, I reminded myself of the vow I had made to keep him happy and healthy for a good long while. Of course it was always difficult to convince myself of the "healthy" part of it whenever Cooper paced around in recovery from a seizure, but then he would be all Cooper again—every bit the happy-go-lucky, playful, beautiful, and loving puppy he had always been. He always ate well, always had plenty of time to play, and he lived with a mom who adored him. Now he would get to do all those same things in my childhood home and would have two people to care for him where before he had one. Every seventeenth day wasn't pretty for him. But during the sixteen days in between, he lived and would continue to live every dog's dream. As long as that was the case, I knew I had to keep fighting for him. Even if I had to leave him behind for a while, I would do whatever it took to keep him going.

That process began by visiting the local animal hospital so I could introduce myself and familiarize the vets with Cooper's case. That local hospital turned out to be a small clinic in Allison Park, a north suburb of Pittsburgh. Let's say the vet's name was Dr. Kate Donaldson, and that she was a kind-eyed, assured woman who took to Cooper immediately. I explained the situation, and she agreed that leaving Cooper in the States was the best possible solution for him.

"You don't know what kind of care they have down there yet. So it's probably best if you figure out the lay of the land before you move him again."

I thanked her for that insight because it helped me alleviate more of the guilt. Leaving Cooper was the last thing I wanted to do, but everyone I spoke to insisted that it was the right thing to do.

"But I just can't shake this thought about what happens if he has a really bad seizure and I'm not here," I said.

Dr. Donaldson gave a thoughtful nod. "That can be tough. And I can see that you're really dedicated to Cooper here." She offered him a playful pat on the side and ruffled his ears. "What I think you need is some assurance that if his time comes, he'll be taken care of."

I agreed. "But how do I get that?"

"Have you considered a living will?"

At the time, I'd never even *heard* of a living will. But Dr. Donaldson explained that it was a legal-ish document that granted power of care to the people and vets of my choosing during the time I would be away. It would outline my expectations for how his care would be managed and would help grant me peace of mind that everyone was on the same page about how to manage the unthinkable inevitability that was Cooper's last big seizure.

"I assume you won't be reachable in St. Kitts all the time," Dr. Donaldson said.

"Probably not. I don't know what the Internet or phone situation is down there."

"Well then a living will makes even more sense in this case. This way, if we can't reach you, we know exactly what you want us to do."

I sighed with relief and thanked the doctor. It was clear that she cared about our situation, and that she would do whatever it took to serve as Cooper's veterinary champion in my place, should a life-or-death situation ever arise during the four long months I would be away for my first semester. It felt good to know that we had added another ally to Team Cooper. Now all I had to do was figure out how to summarize my expectations for his care into a single document. The guy had a complicated situation, and my feelings about how to manage it were so conflicted that I wasn't even sure whether *I* would know what to do if Cooper's life—or even his *quality* of life— ever seemed threatened by his condition.

My parents' basement would serve as the setting. There, on that old desktop computer with the bubble screen, I would get to work on summarizing Cooper's end-of-life care. It's strange to write something like this when the one you're writing it about is curled up on a pile of blankets just beside you. It's stranger still to know that the one you're writing it about has no idea what's going on. Plus, we're talking about a living, breathing being that has only experienced just over a year of life. I was typing out instructions for how to manage the end of that short life, and Cooper remained totally oblivious. As my fingers worked the keys, he snored contentedly at my feet.

Partly because of that strange circumstance, and partly because of the tears and anguish that came with every sentence, it took me a long while to synthesize my thoughts into a single page of uncomfortably dispassionate legal-ish text. But eventually I managed to break it down like so:

Cooper's Living Will
Owner: Katti Ann Strahsmeier

I, Katti Strahsmeier, herby give my consent to perform any procedures within reason needed to help my dog, Cooper, an English Foxhound, live a healthy, good quality life. If he becomes more ill after I leave the US on August 26, 2002, I still want to continue on any medications that will help control his seizures or keep him healthy. I want to do everything I can to help him live a good, long life.

However, if he becomes too ill and his quality of life is no longer of a fair status, which is stated outright by the veterinarian, then I give my consent to have Cooper euthanized and buried in a pet cemetery.

However, I want to be contacted before this event is to occur, unless he is seizuring uncontrollably for an extended period of time in which he would be brain damaged and I am unable to be reached by telephone or through email. I also give Dr. Matthew McCormick DVM my consent and trust to make the judgment call, according to what I have stated in this will, on having to euthanize Cooper in my absence (if you cannot get a hold of me).

Signed,

Katti Ann Strahsmeier

It felt like I'd been sitting working at that document for hours, even though it had probably only been ten minutes or so. I got up from the tiny felt office chair and went to the door that led from the basement into the driveway to take a look outside. Cooper followed me, his breath warm on my leg as I stared into the darkness outside. I'm not sure why, but I was reminded of that dragonfly, and the symbol of Cooper's longevity brought me a moment of peace. I decided that we could both use a walk to clear our heads, so I hooked Cooper to his extendable leash and let him fly outside.

As we wandered around the front and back yards, he bounded like a deer, all playful and giddy to be in the great outdoors. He would run to the end of his line and sniff around, then return to me, his tongue wagging, his ears flopping from side to side.

"Oh, Coop."

He looked at me expectantly as my hand went to scratch the top of his head. Then he slid past and nuzzled my thigh. I knelt and took his head in my arms, hugging him.

"We'll get this figured out, won't we, buddy?"

He seemed to agree.

Back in the basement, I printed the document and signed it.

The time between completing Cooper's living will and having to start packing for St. Kitts seemed to fly by in an instant. It was as though that document allowed me the semblance of closure I needed to start focusing on the exciting life ahead of me. Still, every moment I spent with Cooper I did my best to cherish. Just like with Amy, I didn't want to admit that this would be the last time I would see him for a long while. I tried not to think that this might be the last time I would ever see him.

Then came another one of those moments where I had to worry that it would in fact be the last time I would ever see him. On Dr. Donaldson's advice, I decided to have Cooper neutered before I left. She had made the suggestion in the belief that neutering him might cut down on his seizures. Now this is something that many, many dogs go through when they're puppies, but most of them don't have the kind of neurological issues that put them at risk of having an adverse reaction to anesthesia. So if it had been any other puppy, I wouldn't have worried about the minor risks associated with the procedure. With Cooper, those risks were more than minor.

So on the day of his surgery, I went from worrying that I wouldn't see him again before my semester was over to worrying that I wouldn't see him again in a matter of hours. It all turned out okay, but then Cooper wound up on another set of drugs to help him deal with the pain and healing. This would only make managing his care more difficult for my parents.

In the lead-up to my departure, every chance I got, I steered my parents back to the reassuring conversation about how this was only temporary—that Cooper would only be here for the first semester so I could see how vet school and life in St. Kitts worked. They always volunteered their encouragement and reiterated that this was only a temporary parting.

"We'll take good care of him," Dad kept saying. "You don't need to worry about Cooper at all."

"You just worry about your studies," Mom would echo.

I agreed that this would be for the best, and yet, in the final days before my flight, I couldn't stop talking to my parents about how to care for Cooper. It was a complicated regimen of feeding and pill-giving and seizure-watching and vet-taking. I just wanted to make sure that they had committed everything to memory before I left. I trusted my parents completely, but at the same time, I didn't want to leave my best friend with someone unprepared for the weight of his care.

And the specter of what would happen if ever he had the big seizure while I was unreachable hung over me like a rain cloud.

"Why don't you write all this down?" my mom suggested. "That way, you'll know that if we ever have any questions, we can just look at your instructions."

I took to this suggestion with vigor. The care instructions I wrote were so detailed and so particular that I've kept them for all these years, just so I can get in a good laugh at myself from time to time. In the interest of brevity, I'll just mention that I typed out four full pages of bulleted instructions with frequent lapses into ALL-CAPS URGENCY. They outlined Cooper's hour-by-hour feeding and treat schedule, covered some entirely too detailed directions on how to give him his monthly heartworm medications, and then passed through more than two pages of play-by-play on his almost comically intricate medications routine and THE MANY THINGS YOU SHOULD AND SHOULDN'T DO IN THE EVENT OF A SEIZURE. I went completely overboard on the color coding. My parents learned that they would need to manage Cooper's phenobarbital, his potassium bromide, and even his valium, the latter administered in the event that he needed help pulling out of a seizure. Rolling up a pill in some cheese or peanut butter three times a day and popping it into Cooper's mouth is one thing, but imagine having to administer 10ml of Diazepam by needle-less syringe straight to your daughter's dogs rectum—or as I wrote in the care instructions document, "squirting it into his rectum (butthole) slowly."

On top of all this, my parents would now need to become experts in seizure counting, seizure severity, and seizure duration. I explained that they should expect a similar pattern of episodes to emerge every seventeen days, and that any departure from the usual seizure routine would be an indication that they should

"CALL THE VETERINARIAN!!!" or "TAKE HIM IMMEDIATELY TO THE HOSPITAL – HOURS: 8:00AM-8:00PM."

I still can't imagine what my parents must have thought upon reading this intimidatingly detailed thing. Volunteering to assume the care of a dog with severe seizures is one thing. But volunteering to hold the stopwatch during those seizures, clap-and-yell to keep a dog from slipping too far into an episode, and inject a controlled substance into a dog's butthole? These are entirely different things. Plus, the instructions were so intricate; I not only listed all the emergency contact numbers but also committed the page space to explaining how to use the automated touchtone menu system on the phone. I can just see my parents rolling their eyes, but what can I say? I cared a great deal about Cooper, so I didn't want to leave even one little thing to chance.

"I am trying to do everything I can do to keep my puppy alive and well," I wrote. "I hope you do too!"

So this was how I left the matter in my parents' hands. I burdened them with these instructions, a living will, a red-and-cream-colored bag full of veterinary drugs, my meticulous records about Cooper's seizures, and further care instructions. And of course, the package also came with one puppy named Cooper.

My beautiful dog was fully healthy and happy on the day I left for the airport. I didn't want to lose it on him—or on my parents—so I tried to focus on the details of his care as a distraction from the emotional toll of my departure. I must have rambled on about his dosage and feeding schedule about thirty times through before my parents finally urged me to say my goodbyes so we could get to the airport.

There in the kitchen, Cooper seemed to sense that something was different. When I knelt in front of him, his big, soft paws slid over my shoulders, the weight of him pressing into my chest. We stood there together in the closest thing to a proper embrace that a woman and a dog can share. He sniffed at my face as if wanting to make sure he would remember my smell. I lowered him down and knelt to his level.

"Goodbye, Cooper. You be a good boy, okay?"

He seemed to understand.

"I love you," I said. "I'll see you in a little bit. I'll be right back." I always told him that.

$$\bullet \ \bullet \ \bullet$$

Every moment up to touchdown in St. Kitts, I struggled with a numb, uneasy feeling. At first, I thought it was the kind of anxiousness that comes with any life-changing trip. I figured maybe it was from a mixture of not knowing what to expect from my new school and home and a little of that nagging feeling that I'd forgotten to pack something important. But then, as soon as we arrived at the gate and the rush of all that newness came crowding in, I realized I had been wrong all along. I was excited and nervous about setting up a new life in a new country, yes, but that numb uneasiness was actually from missing Cooper. Obviously, I missed my parents and friends too, but missing them came with the buffer of certainty that I would see them all again one day. With Cooper, there was that heavy weight in my heart that I might have just hugged him for the last time.

I didn't want to think about the inevitability of my dog's death, so I dug in and focused on navigating the comically small, bus-station-esque airport that was Robert Llewellyn Bradshaw International Airport in St. Kitts. It didn't take me long to find my bags on the conveyor belt—and this was entirely because they were enormous. At the time, the airline allowed any checked bag to weigh as much as one hundred pounds. When I'd first set them on the scale back at the Pittsburgh airport's check-in desk, one of them had exceeded that weight while the other was a couple dozen pounds lighter. With my parents' help, I had scrambled to move everything around to where both bags weighed exactly one hundred pounds. The check-in agent had rolled her eyes at me as if this weren't the first time she had seen such a maneuver, but she would be glad if it were the last. The bags sagged so much from the weight that she had to call over some help to flop them onto the belt. I could only imagine the hernias they had caused the baggage handlers charged with hurling them into the belly of the plane.

As I stared at them there at the baggage claim in St. Kitts, it occurred to me that now I would have to haul them around on my own. When I wrenched the first bag off the belt, I had the notion that I probably looked like an emperor penguin waddling belly-first to pass my delicate egg. Fortunately, I would have help with the second bag. It came in the form of an unassuming country girl from North Carolina named Jen. We had met during the layover in Puerto Rico, and after talking for a while, it dawned on us that we were both heading to St. Kitts for vet school, and that in fact, we would be roommates.

The two of us clicked immediately. She wore her wavy brown hair past her shoulders and could always charm with that southern twang. She had a sunny disposition and a tremendous laugh. She used that laugh as she wriggled in beside me and we worked together to yank my second gigantic bag off the conveyor belt. It was such a chore that it nearly threw us off balance. If not for the sturdy stance of the local man standing to my left, we'd have toppled to the floor in a cackling heap.

Ross University had set up the flight itineraries for each of their incoming veterinary students, so for the most part, we were all there at customs at the same time. I looked around and saw dozens of faces that would become quite familiar to me in the ensuing months and years. On that day, our faces all carried the same nervous anticipation as we shuffled downstairs and waited for the shuttle vans that the school's itinerary had promised us.

When the vans started arriving, we met with a tour guide, a Ross student the school had sent us to get oriented. She was blonde and stout and pretty, and of all places, she was from my hometown of Pittsburgh. The moment we realized the connection, I felt a great deal of the anxiety about being in this dramatically new place dissipate. She explained that she would show us around the island for a bit before delivering each of us to the residences we would call home. They packed about a dozen students per van, along with their luggage, which made for some pretty sluggish transport vehicles. When they slung my bags into the back, I could see that the weight would test the mettle of the van's rickety suspension.

As we boarded the van, our Pittsburghian tour guide handed out some welcome packets and told us that we would have plenty of time to get familiar with them prior to our orientation at the school. Then she slid into the passenger seat, and the driver took off.

We rumbled over craggy roads through hilly terrain, the sun-splashed Caribbean waters very much in sight to the west. I couldn't wait to see everything the island had to offer and learn everything I could from the tour.

"You know what?" the tour guide said. "You're all here. Why don't we take you to get something to eat? Then we'll do a quick run of the island and get you to your houses."

I was so excited to be in this new place that I hadn't noticed how hungry I was. At the mention of food, my stomach started to roar so loudly I was sure the others could hear it. Tucked in shoulder to shoulder with my fellow students, I couldn't help but grin. I was here. This would be the place I would call home for the next eighteen months. Prior to visiting this island for the first time, I had assumed that the pictures I found online were merely the most flattering angles of the locale—propaganda from the St. Kitts' tourism department. As I took it in now, I was struck by how I couldn't have been more wrong. No matter which way I looked, St. Kitts presented as something straight out of Microsoft Windows desktop wallpaper. I could already sense that I would love it here.

That's when everything started getting real. Downtown was a surprisingly bustling little hamlet of Spanish architecture done up in tropical island pastels. Pedestrians ruled the streets from the residential outskirts, through the commercial districts, and all the way to the long, broad port that jutted out over the pristine blue-green waters. The driver parked the van in a tightly packed lot on the east end of town, and from there, we all wound our way into the crowds. We'd been instructed to keep close together, because the locals would sometimes hassle the more obvious tourists. As pasty and sun-screened as the majority of us were, we could not have fit that description more completely.

I wanted to sample some of the local fare, and to enjoy something genuinely St. Kitts on my first day in town, but we wound up herding to the only fast-food place on the island because our tour guides seemed to be in a hurry. That's how I wound up eating KFC as my first meal in my new home.

I'd only just gotten back to my table with my two-piece meal of fried chicken parts when the Pittsburgher dropped the bomb on us.

"Welcome to the island," she said. "Some of you might have noticed that your numbers are a little short."

We all looked around wide-eyed as if to say, "Really? I hadn't noticed. Who's missing?"

She sighed. "The school has asked me to talk to you about this because it's a matter of your safety." She shook her head as if mourning something she couldn't quite bring herself to talk about. "One of your classmates arrived a day earlier than the rest of you. Last night, she was lured out of her apartment by a local man." She clenched her teeth as if willing herself to say what had to be said. Then, suddenly, she straightened up and spoke about it all as if it were the easiest thing in the world. "She was raped."

A chill crept up my spine as the lot of us started murmuring through our disbelief.

"Obviously, this student isn't going to be part of your class anymore. And obviously that's not the impression we want to give you about your new home. I can tell you firsthand that this isn't a typical thing. It's the first time it's happened to anyone since I've been here. But at the same time, you shouldn't take it lightly."

More murmuring.

Our guide held up a calming hand, and we quieted down. "Just be careful, okay. Don't go out of your apartments at night. Ladies, be sure to travel in groups at all times. Violent crime isn't common on the island, but it isn't exactly uncommon either, if you know what I mean."

We all started nodding. It wasn't the kind of thing we wanted to hear on our first day in paradise. The sudden fear for my safety coupled with the culture shock to make the rest of the settling-in process entirely surreal. Even though I had just spent a summer in Pennsylvania getting used to the warmth, the heat on the island felt less like a typical late August and more like the inside of a car that had just spent all day in the sun of a typical late August. There is summer-hot, and then there is summer-on-a-Caribbean-island-hot. There's just no comparison. Of course it didn't help that the shuttle van's cooling system had depended on wet heat pumped through open windows, and there was no a/c in my new home. Upon first setting foot in that new home, I had a mind to take a cold shower just to get the scorch of the climate out of my bones, but there was too much to do.

The surroundings were decidedly beautiful, if a little rustic compared to what I was used to. Having to find a pack to travel with whenever I left the house made for a different perspective on getting by. It was always comforting to have the company and support of my new classmates, but I could see that the specter of the rape was going to hang over all of us, at least until we got comfortable with how life worked on the island.

Eventually, I got to try the local food. It was exotic and gritty and entirely different from anything I'd had before. The amenities were a little lacking too. Phone, Internet, and television were all unreliable. Whenever I needed an item I took for granted back home, there weren't any Targets or CVSs on the island to hook me up. I had to learn to deal with perceived shortages pretty quickly. Also, the pace of life was slow—cement-drying-slow, *impossibly* slow. It was so slow that the local motto had evolved into "rush slowly." So whenever I had to get something done that involved intervention from any of the locals, I had to expect that it would take far longer than it ever would back home. Something that would take a few minutes in the States would often take several days in St. Kitts.

Not that I had any reason to complain. Against the odds, I had gotten into vet school, and I was going to be studying on a tropical island that most jet-setting Americans only ever see as part of a stop on a cruise ship. The place where I would conduct my studies would be one that thousands and thousands of people thought of as a genuine paradise. In all corners, one could find a beach or a pool. I never had to go far to find a Carib beer or a piña colada to cool my hand. There was always a beach volleyball game I could join. Plus, my new friends and I lived near a strip of bars and clubs on the beach that offered plenty of opportunity for late nights and uproarious times. Inon's was a favorite stop, given that it was essentially just a shack with a dance floor, and it was run by a tall, improbably skinny, dreadlocked-to-the-waist, typically shoeless, and constantly stoned Rasta named Inon. Shiggidy Shack was another place. Good spot to hang out and dance.

At the center of my new little paradise was the compound in which I lived. That was the way of the world on St. Kitts: just about everyone lived in compounds of multiple houses surrounded by tall fortification walls usually accessed by a slow-sliding front gate. I lived in a compound with three houses. I shared my house with Jen, while my landlord lived with his mother in the house to our left, and my landlord's brother lived in another house to our right. The place rested right on the Caribbean, its grassy yard giving way to a meadow, then a craggy outcrop, and finally, a cliff that descended several meters into the sea. The view was proper spectacular. Almost every night, I could look up from studying to see a cruise ship or two either arriving or leaving port, their lights blending with the unimaginable number of stars one can see from a vantage so close to open water.

The house itself was a fairly drab joint, with its whitewashed walls and brown shutters, its dark porch and roof, its white tile floors, and its tacky décor. The yard was where the true inspiration checked in—all sea views and banana, avocado, and mango trees. Our landlord had provided an array of rickety furniture centered by an old, grungy couch. Even though it had its quirks, I loved every square inch of that place. The only problem was that Cooper didn't live there.

For canine companionship, there was Spike, my landlord's dog, but he was a Chow mix and just plain nasty to anyone he didn't know. It took him a long while to warm to the new guests in the house. Spike had a puppy named Blossom who was cute and much sweeter. Then there was Jake, my roommate Jen's handsome Rhodesian Ridgeback with the short, sad story of how he'd lost his trademark ridge of fur and had it replaced with a disfiguring scar that ran the length of his back.

It was nice to have dogs around, but none of them was Cooper.

Fortunately, the new people in my life were excellent company. Jen was good to have around because she made for a calming, driven sort of friend. One hundred percent of the reason she was on this island was to go to school. I dug that about her, even though I couldn't relate to a preference to keep to the books every waking hour when there was so much joy to be had and friends to be made out in the big, fun world.

Every day, the two of us would carpool from the compound to our classes. We would usually grab some breakfast sandwiches—almost always bacon, egg, and cheese sandwiches lovingly crafted by Neil himself—at Neil's Café on campus. Then we'd file in for classes from 8am to 3pm every day. Afterward, we would come home, where Jen would go off to study in her room while I relaxed with some TV for a bit before retreating to the dining room table to enjoy some coconut cookies, a Coke made with real sugarcane, and my own hours-long study session. Sometimes I would hit the sack after that. Other times, I would go out to enjoy the nightlife. Either way, there was always a sugarcane Coke in an old-timey glass bottle and some coconut cookies. Couldn't study without them.

I would buy my treats at a funny little place just down the block. "OOJJ's," it was called—no periods necessary for those mysterious initials. OOJJ's played Bob Marley on a constant loop and would play it so loudly that often we could hear it all the way from our house. They sold fried chicken and fried fish out of a drive-or-walk-thru window on the right-hand side, and on the left-hand side, they turned wrenches in a rundown car repair shop. I never had any need for these fine services, but they saw me almost every day on my cookie and Coke order.

I tended to pick up my friends on those nights when I would venture out. My best friend Timi and I met at a party on the beach when we both happened to have to pee at the same time and chose to squat on the same sand dune.

Then there were Amanda, Laura, and Randa, three friends I met while on a school-sponsored catamaran trip. The boat took us to Sunshine's, a famous bar often associated with the island. The bartenders at Sunshine's make a drink called a Killer Bee, the recipe for which they keep a closely guarded secret. No one knows what's in it, but it will completely and utterly destroy you. I learned that lesson the hard way, and so did my three new friends. I don't remember much about the night, save for snippets. There was dancing on the bar with the natives. There was hanging off the side of the catamaran in our bikinis. There was a car I didn't recognize. There was utter terror about driving on the left side of the road. There were the locals we dropped off at various houses. I'm pretty sure I kissed a guy named Carlos.

In hindsight, none of it makes much sense, but it does help explain—at least in part—why, out of the one-hundred-and-six people in my unusually large class, only eighty would graduate. From those eighty, I would make some of the best friends a vet student could ask for. Some had gone to VT like me, but others were from all over the country. In this way, the cultural education I received on the island was peppered with the cultural educations I received from friends who had grown up in places like Texas, California, Virginia, Miami, and Puerto Rico. Alongside these people, I would do things like clack away in the computer lab, peer into microscopes, hit the books, and dissect a donkey. We would endure the hissing from the locals who wanted our attention, and the other women and I would stand up for each other during the local men's shockingly aggressive sexual advances. Then there were impromptu parties, Halloween parties, and even a party with an Olympic theme involving various alcohol-fueled pseudo-sporting events on the beach.

Life was genuinely and truly good. Except that I constantly missed Cooper.

My only connection to Cooper and the world back home was via my computer. This was pre-Skype and even pre-affordable-international-cellphones, so back then, AOL Instant Messenger was all the rage. I can still hear the staccato spleedles and sploops of a typical AIM conversation, can still remember how my heart would race whenever a message I was waiting patiently for finally came through. And wait patiently is exactly what I often had to do. The Internet in my new home was dial-up, and the phone lines unreliable. This meant that I would have to send a message, then wait for minutes and agonizing minutes for it to finally go through and then return with a reply.

Eventually I picked up some headphones and a webcam I could talk into, but the connection was never strong enough for the video, and the headphones and microphone were so spotty that I usually just resorted to text. I would instant message with my friends, of course, but the conversations I looked forward to the most were the Sunday evening variety with my parents. We would spend maybe an hour catching up on all the goings on in our separated lives, and I would always be thirsty for as much information as possible on Cooper's health and wellbeing.

Most conversations were fine, but some were terrifying. Some featured a painfully slow back and forth about how Cooper had been seizing for the past few days. Then there was the one where Cooper had an episode while we were chatting.

"Oh, he's having a seizure," my mom wrote.

My heart stopped. I felt suddenly boxed in by my tiny, windowless room on an island in the middle of the sea.

"Oh my God. It's so bad," Mom added.

I broke into a cold sweat, my fingers suddenly stiff as I fumbled with the keys. "What?! How bad?" I wrote. Then, when several minutes passed with no reply, I was left wondering whether it was a connection issue or my mom had to step away from the keyboard to try to keep my dog from seizing so hard he never got up again. I knew that my sister Heidi and her husband Pete were visiting my parents that night, so it helped to know that there was at least one nurse and an additional strong man in the house at the time, but the wait remained agony.

"What's happening?!" I wrote into the void. "Are you still there, Mom?"

"He's in the yard," came the cryptic reply.

Then my phone line went out and AIM switched off. Panic rose up my spine, forcing me to my feet and causing me to scream at my computer screen. "What do you mean he's in the yard?" I typed uselessly. The message would never go through. Frantically I turned in circles in my tiny room, looking for a solution I knew I could never solve with my own two hands. Still, I went to the cable that connected my modem to the phone outlet, unplugging it and plugging it back in. I tried logging back on to the connection, and then to Instant Messenger, to no avail.

I briefly pondered rebooting my computer, but that old brick would've taken ten minutes to fire back up again.

And so I waited. And I imagined the worst. My eyes started to water. My hands began to shake.

Then, against all odds, the connection returned, and with it, full audio from the other end of the line. My mom must not have realized I had cut out, because she was still in mid-freakout when her voice came shrilly through my headphones.

"He's in the neighbor's yard. Oh my God! We're trying to help him, but we can't get him back in the house!"

I started screaming things back at her, but I was so wigged out myself that I don't remember anything I might have said. It was surely nothing useful, because what could I have done from an ocean away? I had a deeper knowledge of how Cooper's seizures looked and how to mitigate them, but when a seizure starts happening, the only thing that helps is physical strength and emotional resolve from the caregiver, and from where I sat in that tiny, white-walled box of a room, I could offer neither of those things. All I could manage was hysterics and wild text messages full of typos.

"Kepe his heed protect," I mistyped, meaning that it was most important that they move any objects he could smash his head into. I screamed something to this effect, as well, but wasn't sure whether either message went through.

There is no way to describe how helpless I felt. I had seen Cooper seize more times than I could reasonably recall and had always found the experiences emotionally overwhelming. Every time one happened, I would rush in and help him in the ways I had been taught, and every time they were over, I always felt so exhausted inside and out from the sheer intensity and length of them. To know that someone else had to step in for me made the emotional exhaustion even deeper. And the waiting for reply magnified everything even further. The five or so minutes it took for my connection to return felt like two days and ten seconds all at the same time.

"We got him," my mom wrote. "He's okay."

Relief washed over me, but not full relief—more like the hollow kind of relief that comes when you learn that the first wave is over, but there are more waves to come. Cooper had gotten through this particularly terrible seizure, but there would be other seizures similar to earthquake aftershocks that would show up over the next twenty-four hours.

My mom and I spent the next ten minutes or so catching me up on all that had happened that night. Cooper had been out in the yard when it started. Pete had seen him, and by the time anyone could get out to Cooper, he was already in the neighbor's yard. The neighbors had come out as well, but everyone had been forced to stand around helplessly as Pete tried to keep Cooper as still as possible. By the time we finished chatting, my dog was up and walking around normally again, but we all knew it was just a matter of time before another seizure would come. And if this one had been as bad as my mom said it was, then I had to believe the next seizure could be worse.

In some ways, bad news is not nearly as difficult to cope with as not fully knowing the extent of the bad news. Had I been present for that seizure in the neighbor's yard, I might not have felt so wretched. At least I'd have been able to see it with my own eyes and process the experience on my own. But with this new living situation, I had to get everything third-hand. I would learn about his incidents from two people who meant well, but who didn't have all the facts at the ready. They would learn information from Cooper's vets, then have trouble relating the full details back to me. They would watch Cooper seize, and then not be able to describe the differences from one seizure to the next in quite the same detail I might have gleaned had I been there.

No matter where the communication broke down, three things were clear: first, Cooper's seizures were getting worse. Second, it wasn't fair for me to think that my parents could handle this responsibility on their own anymore. And finally, I could no longer bear to live apart from my dog. I had vowed that I would give him the best life possible and help him live comfortably and happily for as long as he was physically, mentally, and emotionally capable of being comfortable and happy. It was abundantly clear now that I couldn't do that when we lived apart. So I waited out the last couple of weeks of the semester and then returned home with a mind to retrieve him.

CHAPTER SIX

Baggage Claim

My journey would start and end with an airplane. The start featured an excitement so deep, it permeated the whole of me, warming me to the point where I felt I didn't even need a jacket after landing at Pittsburgh International Airport smack in the middle of December.

Dad's was the first familiar face I saw. He gave a soft smile when he caught my eye. Then he nudged the person next to him, and when she turned around, I saw my mother.

"My God, you're so tan!" she said as she ran up to greet me.

I beamed and hugged her. Then I hugged my dad.

"Let's get you home," Dad said.

"Your friend can't wait to see you," Mom said.

I felt all tingly at the thought of reuniting with Cooper.

When I first saw him again in the flesh—or in the silky fur, as it were—he was quiver-bounding inside his crate, the kind of frenetic, excited movement that only a puppy can pull off. My dad's smile was the broad, hopeful kind that so matched what I felt in my heart. The warmth of the basement served a stark contrast to the considerable cold outside, but I didn't even notice it as I unlatched the crate and hugged and kissed my giddy best friend.

My parents and I laughed as Cooper wriggled and writhed against my coat, trying to get as close to me as he could. His tongue hung, his eyes projecting an intense, glassy joy. I couldn't stop hugging him. I was just so excited and relieved. My dreams—both the night and the daydream variety—had been plenty dark over those final two weeks of the semester. I'd been living with this consistent, humming dread that I was so close to coming home and reuniting with my dog, but wouldn't make it quite in time. On that final night before my departure from St. Kitts, I dreamed of Cooper's upcoming second birthday, and I dreamed of his final day. I'd woken that morning to a chill that made no sense on a tropical island which, even in December, promised a humid 85 degrees pretty much 24/7. That weird chill had never left me even as I made the long flight home.

But now I was with my family. Now I had Cooper at my side. My insides had warmed up again, even as the temperatures outside plunged into the twenties.

The culture shock on the return trip was much less considerable. I buried myself in the happy comfort of being back with the people I loved, and of having all those conveniences I had learned to live without on the island. The weather sucked, but none of that mattered because we had a glowing hearth and everyone had tucked into that familial Christmas warmth that comes with every Pittsburgh December. The holidays reunited me with family and friends, with my amazing sisters and their husbands, and with the sense that all would be well in the world as long as I could always come back home. Everything was familiar and loving and absolutely right. Even though it had only been a temporary home for me, my basement room felt more homelike than the house at St. Kitts could ever possibly feel. The welcome familiarity of all my old haunts filled me with a gladness so intensely rewarding that I could hardly contain it. Even my Jeep—rendered a crispy, frosted hunk of metal from its idle months in the driveway—was like a long-lost friend.

Christmas was there and gone with blinding rapidity, and suddenly I was facing down the barrel of the notion that my break was almost halfway over. I reassured myself that, no matter how fleeting the time felt, I was going to make the most of it.

The date was December 29th, 2002. Cooper's second birthday. By then, my family and friends had become quite familiar with my uncommon bond with Cooper—enough so that they didn't seem at all surprised that I wanted to throw him a big birthday bash. This was the second one I'd held for him, after all. As corny as I'm sure most of the attendees thought his first birthday party was, this time, it was going to be even cornier and more emotional for me. This was the first birthday Cooper would celebrate after getting his grim diagnosis. This was the first milestone following the vow I had made to keep him living happily and comfortably for as long as I could.

"Where is it you're going again?" my mom asked as I grabbed the keys to the Jeep.

"Shop N' Save," I called back as I headed for the stairs.

"What'd you forget?" This in reference to how we had already been to the grocery store a couple of times in preparation for the party.

I paused at the top of the stairs. "Nothing. I just have to pick up the cake."

"But we're *baking* the cake."

"We're baking the cake for the *people*." I tried not to sound too loony. "I had the bakery at the grocery store make the cake for Cooper."

She gave me a perplexed look. "*Cooper* is having cake too?"

"Yeah." I shrugged.

"Aren't dogs supposed to, you know…*avoid* sugar?"

I laughed. "I wouldn't let him have cake if I knew it would make him sick. He might poop funny a few hours later. But wait'll you see him dig into the thing. It's *adorable* how much he loves it."

I didn't need to stick around to see my mother's smiling eye-roll. I could feel it. I *understood* it, too, because even I had to admit that wanting to give my dog his own cake placed me a little closer to the border of nutjob dog-mom than I typically preferred to reside. But I took comfort in the knowledge that, since the lady who took the order for Cooper's cake didn't flinch at the idea, it must have meant I wasn't the only person in town going to these lengths to celebrate her dog.

While at the store, I made sure to pick up one of those little candles shaped like a "2."This would go on the people cake. I'd light it and we would sing to him. I would probably be the only one singing with any semblance of vigor, but so what? Cooper was my big, two-year-old boy. He'd outlived all expectations—*doubled them*, even—and as far as I was concerned, this would be just the first of many milestone years and many days to continue outliving those expectations.

I spent the rest of the morning setting up the cakes, wrapping Cooper's presents—a random assortment of chew toys from the pet store, and a brand-new collar designed to make him feel more comfortable as he tugged me along the street on one of his walk/stalks after a scent that led him in endless, random directions—dressing the table in a decorative cloth and birthday-themed center-piece, and assembling the party favors.

The turnout was predictably small but loving. My parents and sisters were in attendance, as was my brother-in-law, Pete. My mom and sisters weren't quite as into dogs as my dad and me, so they wore their party hats mostly just to humor their nutty daughter/sister, and they sang with halfhearted cheer. My dad, though, was completely into it. He lit the candle for me and followed me into the kitchen as we sang "Happy Birthday" to Cooper while I carried the cake. When we were finished, I set the cake in front of Cooper as if to let him blow it out. He looked at the flame for a moment, squinting in confusion. Then he licked the air a couple of times. I cackled, then blew out his candle.

Everyone gave a mock cheer.

Dad cut the cake while I helped Cooper open his birthday presents. I wanted him to open them himself, so I guided his paw around to help him pull the wrapping apart. Every time he got one of the toys out, he went bananas, snatching it up in his mouth and wriggling around the floor with it. We all laughed and beamed down at him, and he seemed to drink in our affection. He would reel back from his new toy and sit regally, his tongue waggling as if the attention were the most marvelous thing he could possibly imagine.

There is nothing better than a good dog.

When the time came for me to give him his cake, he wasted no time wolfing it down.

"I'd say he likes it," my mom said, still sounding a little incredulous that we were feeding him cake.

Cooper finished, and when he looked up, he gave me a contented, frosting-smeared smile before rolling onto his side and panting off the pastry bliss. He stayed there, surrounded by his toys and wrapping paper and the massacred remains of the cake, for a long while.

• • •

Several weeks before I was due to return to St. Kitts, I began the process of preparing Cooper to come to the island with me. While it was a convoluted process, it was well worth it because I just couldn't stand the thought of being apart from him for another day, let alone another semester. My mom seemed pretty relieved that I'd decided to stick to the original plan and take Cooper back with me. I was getting a decidedly "Get him out of here" vibe from her. I couldn't blame her. My dog was more than a handful.

American Airlines was willing to allow my dog to fly—fortunately, as they were the only airliner that served St. Kitts. The notion that he would have to ride in the cargo hold terrified me, and for a minute, gave me pause about bringing him along at all, but then I weighed the prospect of a day of having to be sedated in the belly of a plane against several months of not being under the care of the person who wanted most desperately to keep him happy and healthy. This would be my last trip home for quite some time—for over a year, maybe—so it seemed like now or never.

There was a process for registering with the USDA and applying to take Cooper out of the country with me. St. Kitts was a rabies-free island, so it would prove difficult to get Cooper from a place familiar with rabies to a place where the disease didn't exist. I had to subject him to blood tests, which his vet then shipped to Kansas State University, who would examine them, report on them, and ship them back in a procedure that took four to six weeks. In the interim, there was loads of paperwork with which to contend. I also scheduled a drive to Harrisburg, PA, on the other side of the state to meet with a USDA officer who presented a handful of additional forms for me to sign. We had to clear a long series of bureaucratic hurdles and set up all kinds of veterinary care to occur both in the US before our departure and in St. Kitts after our arrival. The whole process was not unlike applying for a visa.

I also had to correspond with the airline about Cooper's specific ailments and care. I explained that he had severe allergies and needed to get his meds right on time. This was of course a fib, because I knew that if the airline was aware the pills were for seizures, they wouldn't let him fly. And if he had a seizure either in the lead-up to the flight or somewhere before his transfer from one plane to the next during his layover, they wouldn't let him complete the trip. The staff with whom I exchanged emails assured me that everything would be well. I remained skeptical for a few reasons. First, how do you really keep track of a dog when he's in the cargo hold of a plane? Second, over the course of a sixteen-hour flight, how could I trust that there would always be someone around at the proper times to give him his medications?

Those last few days at home passed by with impossible speed. It was like I blinked, and there I was, packing up Cooper and all our belongings for a flight whose prospect made me more nervous with every passing hour.

At Pittsburgh International, I ushered him up to the check-in area, checked us both in, and began the long discussion of the medication procedure with the clerk who would see my dog onto the plane. I made sure to repeat my instructions a couple of times. I pointed out how I had written those same instructions on his crate so everyone along the chain of stops would know what they were supposed to do. I also probably asked the question a dozen different ways, the one about how and when Cooper would be transferred between plane #1 and plane #2 after touchdown in Miami, and then between plane #2 and plane #3 once we were in San Juan. Every time I asked, I received vigorous assurance that everything would go off without a hitch.

"We do this all the time," was the sentiment.

I kept waiting and hoping that someone would add, "And we've never lost a dog," but that particular assurance never came.

Once I was semi-satisfied, I stooped down in front of Cooper's crate, opened the gate, and handed him a treat. Then I checked his water supply and made sure his meds were there in his little carryon.

"It's going to be okay, Coopie," I said, my eyes all watery.

He licked at the bars.

"They'll take good care of you. You just be brave on the flight, okay?"

With a bored little huff, he lay down in his crate and closed his eyes.

"Be a good boy," I said as the clerk started rolling him away. "I love you. I'll be right back."

All through the process of security screening, I carried tension in my shoulders and dread in my heart. I just couldn't shake the feeling that something was about to go terribly wrong. Maybe it was due to the emotional transition of leaving for what promised to be the longest uninterrupted stretch I'd ever been away from home. Maybe I could chalk it all up to standard pre-flight jitters. But the reality was that I worried that something was going to go wrong with Cooper's meds. This made the assuredness I had received from the check-in staff feel less like actual confidence and more like practiced diversions designed to get the customer through the ticketing line as quickly as possible. They had told me they would get my dog to Miami, then switch him to our connecting flight to San Juan, then to our next connecting flight into St. Kitts, and that someone would always be there to pop a pill into him at the appropriate time. I wanted to believe them, but the truth was that I wouldn't *really* believe them until they actually delivered us to our final destination in good health.

The murmur of impatient passengers shuffling through security played as the soundtrack to my anxiety as I removed my shoes and danced the TSA dance. I took the tram to the terminal, then jog-walked over to my gate. I made it just in time to watch through the window as the clerk and a baggage handler wheeled Cooper's crate onto a conveyor belt and loaded him into the plane. My sigh was a nervous one. It felt good to know that he was at least safely on the flight, but there were still so many chances to screw this up. Plus, my poor epileptic dog wasn't exactly going to be spending the next thirteen hours in first class. I didn't want to think about how frightening and uncomfortable it would likely be in that cargo hold. I could only hope that he would sleep as much as possible.

Pittsburgh to Miami proceeded just fine. The moment we landed, I went to the window at the gate and waited until I saw his crate lowered from the plane and moved along with the rest of the baggage. Then I hustled to the nearest American Airlines counter I could find and made them assure me again that Cooper would be routed to San Juan. The clerk was patient with me, and even went through the motions of clacking through her computer for a while, but when she finally assured me that Cooper was indeed en route, I could sense that she wasn't completely certain. No matter. I wasn't at a point of ultimate distrust with the airline staff just yet, so I let it slide and decided to take matters into my own hands.

I jostled through the crisscrossing passengers at Miami airport in search of my gate. There, I had to wait for what felt like an overly long time before the baggage finally started arriving for loading. Cooper's crate was just about the last package to get on board, but the sight of it at least allowed me to perform my second halfhearted sigh of the trip.

Miami to San Juan went off without a hitch. But here there were no windows at my arriving gate that would allow me to watch Cooper get off the flight from Miami, so I couldn't track him on the deplaning. There was a window at the gate for my final flight, but by the time I arrived, they were already loading the luggage, and at no point did I see them put Cooper on the plane. I tried to tell myself that he must have been boarded before I arrived to watch, but I was having a hard time believing it.

The information at the next American Airlines desk proved less forthcoming.

"Are you sure he's on this plane?" I kept asking of the increasingly unsure-looking employees that filed to the computer to check and double-check the apparently fruitless searches.

"Yes, I see that right here," the third woman said as she pointed at a screen I couldn't see from my side of the counter anyway. This clerk wore a tag that informed of her managerial position, but my concern felt no more assuaged by that fact. "He's on the plane." It didn't help that her expression looked decidedly less certain than her words.

"Are you sure?"

Her nod lacked confidence at first, but then when she noticed I was watching her closely, she picked up the pace. "I promise you your dog will be waiting for you in St. Kitts."

"You're sure?"

"One hundred percent," she said with a passive little smile.

Eventually I gave up, figuring that I could at least talk to a flight attendant on the plane to see if he or she could confirm the presence of a large, beautiful, probably super-wired-by-now dog in the cargo hold. So I left the information desk attendants alone and waited for someone to call us in to board.

The plane was comfortable and not terribly crowded, but I couldn't seem to sit still. It took me several tries to flag down one of the busy flight attendants before I finally got an answer. I had to stand in the aisle to bar one of them from ignoring my question and jetting past me.

"Excuse me," I said with a flutter of my eyes. "I was wondering if you could tell me whether my dog was loaded on the plane."

"Yep, he was," the attendant said far too quickly to have thought the question through completely. Then, without changing her plastered-on pleasant expression even a little, she said, "Please sit down."

After the short flight, I rushed through customs. Then I went to the turnstile and waited, bouncing on my feet as the bags started to arrive. Bag after bag came through, but there were absolutely no English Foxhounds. In this way, I was surprised and completely unsurprised to learn that no one at the St. Kitts airport could find my dog. When the first wave of confusion passed, I started freaking the hell out. I don't remember much of what I said or did, but I do know that I left more than a handful of exasperated airline employees genuflecting in my wake.

At some point during the tirade, I pointed out that my luggage had made the trip. I motioned to my gigantic roller bag for proof. "But my dog isn't here. How many people did I talk to about making sure he would get on the flight from San Juan?"

"Um, I don't know, ma'am," said the disarmingly adorable little old man who served American and any number of other airlines in St. Kitts. "But we could place a call to San Juan to see if anyone can help us figure out what happened."

I agreed, then paced away, the tears already starting to fall over my cheeks as he dialed. I was beside myself with a combination of fury and frustration and sorrow, but all of that felt crippled by the sheer weight of my concern for Cooper's safety. When the adorable little old man got through to San Juan, he motioned for me to take the phone, and I practically jumped the ten feet between us in one bound.

"Yes-hi-I'm-looking-for-my-dog-and-he's-not-here-he-was-supposed-to-be-on-the-flight-from-San-Juan-to-St.-Kitts-but-he-wasn't-and-now-we-can't-find-him-and-I'm-freaking-out-please-help-me-find-him."

The voice on the other end of the line played at empathy, but in the end, sounded more bored with work and ready to get home than anything else. There was a long silence interrupted only by the occasional clicking of a keyboard. Then I heard an intake of breath, so I held mine in anticipation of some news.

"Please hold."

Inwardly I groaned, but outwardly I thanked the voice and said okay.

What felt like a year or two passed. I filled it with thoughts of Cooper seizing in the cargo bay somewhere over Cuba, no one there to help secure him or talk him through it.

"Ma'am," the voice said so suddenly it startled me.

"Yes. Yes, I'm here. Please tell me where—"

"Yes, I'm sorry," the voice interrupted. "I'm afraid we can't find any record of your package being loaded onto the flight to St. Kitts."

"He's not a package." I tried not to seethe, but I couldn't help it. "He's my dog. My *dog* didn't get on the plane in San Juan."

"Yes. It looks that way."

"Well, where is he then?"

The discomfort in the short silence that followed was

so thick, I couldn't have smashed it even if I'd had the sledgehammer I suddenly felt the overwhelming urge to start swinging.

"I'm afraid we don't know that as of now."

"As of *now*?"

"We have some of our best people on the job of tracking him down," the voice said, and now there was a hint of genuine sympathy. "The best I can tell you is that we'll call with updates on progress."

"Okay," I said, the word rendered more colorful by the sudden gust of helpless sorrow that breezed through it. I cried there on the phone, not knowing what else to do.

"I'm really sorry, ma'am. I promise they'll find your dog just as quickly as they can."

"He'll need his medication as soon as they do," I said through tears.

"I'll make sure they know that."

By the time I handed the phone back to the little old man, my hand was shaking, and he was all saucer-eyed with concern.

"What did they say?"

"That they'll update me."

He sighed and straightened up. "That is good, I suppose."

We held eye contact for a long while then, my eyes tearful and his soft and grandfatherly. "Do you have anyone you can call?"

I nodded, thanked him, and turned away. Then I called Jaime, a friend of mine from school, and she came to pick me up. It was good to see her. We hugged, and then she helped me get my heavy roller bag into the backseat. I guess I was so nervous and aggravated over the Cooper situation that I failed to notice that the fingers on my left hand were still very much in the path of the back door as I slammed the thing shut with my right. On impact, there was a metallic thump and a noticeable crunch, and the pain rocketed from my knuckles to my spine. It was so searing that I actually had to pause to collect enough energy to scream.

"Are you okay?" Jaime ran around to help me wrench the door open.

At first, I thought they were broken, but I didn't have the energy left to think about that. "I don't know. I don't think so. Let's just get home."

Half fretting, half laughing, we shut the door properly this time and took our seats in the front. My fingers throbbed the whole ride home—and would for the rest of the day, really—but I tried not to think about them. I was too homed in on worrying about whether anyone would ever manage to find my poor puppy. As we drove, I would occasionally steal a glance at my hand, to find that just about everything was black and blue and swollen already. It turned out that I didn't break them, but the pain would still be considerable for the next couple days.

I'm not sure what we did to pass the time that night, but I'm certain there was plenty of literal crying into my beer and zero sleep. I wasn't exactly a smoker, but I know I went through more than my share of cigarettes as well. Nothing helped. Every time the airline called, all they could tell me was that they were still searching. They hadn't found him in baggage claim at San Juan, nor in the sprawling baggage warehouse just outside the airport. Miami was on the job now too, but their search too had turned up fruitless so far. It all felt so surreal. This was a company that managed to successfully transport millions upon millions of bags from one location to another all over the world. It had decades of practice at the fine art of labeling personal belongings, scanning them into a tracking system, and putting them on the correct plane so they could accompany the correct passenger to the correct location. Sure, there would be mistakes from time to time. I'd seen a few of them firsthand. When you have to repeat the same operation millions of times, mistakes just come with the territory.

But, c'mon, how do you lose a 100-pound dog?

Another twelve or so sleepless, semi-drunken hours later, I finally got the call I had been waiting for.

"Ma'am, I have good news. We found your baggage."

"My dog," I corrected again. "Cooper."

"Yes, we found Cooper." This voice sounded more pleased with itself than I felt it should have. All told, it had taken the airline's staff sixteen hours to find my poor puppy. I could only imagine how hungry he was, how badly overdue he was for his medication, and how dire was his need to go to the bathroom.

I was so angrily relieved, I didn't really notice that I had already gotten up and was starting to pick through my suitcase for fresh clothes. "Where is he?"

"He's in San Juan."

Disappointed, I slumped back onto Jaime's couch. I wouldn't be leaving just yet after all.

"But we're routing him to you on the next available plane," the voice added. "That should leave in...let's see..." There was a short silence. "Three hours."

So it would be another six hours at least until I could hold my puppy again.

"Has he been given his medications?"

"Yes." The voice sounded pleasantly sure of itself.

I replied with a doubtful "Thank you," then asked where and when I could plan to meet my poor lost friend. The voice gave me the details, then started the wind-down process that precedes the hang-up.

"Wait," I said. "One more thing."

"Yes?"

"Where did they find him?"

The hesitation that followed was pregnant with embarrassment. "They found him in a closet near the baggage claim in San Juan."

So now I had a picture to go with the fretful sixteen hours he had been missing. He hadn't been circling baggage-claim conveyor belts or circling the blue waters of the Caribbean; he had been sitting silently in a dark closet in some far-flung corner of an airport. A whole team of people had spent sixteen hours trying to track down my dog, and the only reason anyone found him is because a janitor or baggage handler or corporate bureaucrat had some other reason to open that closet door and just stumbled upon him. A whole team scouring the entire baggage operation at two different airports, and someone just goes, "Oh, hey. There's a dog in here."

For the next few, antsy hours of waiting, my anger and

frustration slowly faded into a strange vibe of giddy yet nervous anticipation. I was overjoyed that they had found him finally, but still hugely concerned that he was starving, way behind on his medication, and rocked with the kind of pent-up boredom that could only come from nearly a full twenty-four hours stuck in a crate. I told myself that if they managed to get him to me in one piece and in full health, he and I would spend the next several days just running around outside and the next several nights sharing my bed. As far as I was concerned, dude would never have to see a crate again until it was absolutely necessary.

The airline informed me that there would be an officer with the USDA waiting for me at the airport so he could examine Cooper and give him the clear to spend his first thirty days on the island in quarantine in the compound where I lived. So with Jaime at the wheel again, we roared back to the airport. When we arrived, I went to the desk where I was to meet the officer, and to my great dismay, Cooper wasn't there.

"Have you lost him again?" I wanted to say.

"You're Katti?"

I nodded.

"You got here fast," the woman at the counter said. "He's still on the plane. He should be coming around shortly."

I made uncomfortable conversation with the USDA officer while we waited. He was a tall, unsmiling, almost cartoonishly buff black man named Dr. Henry. I could tell that he wasn't exactly used to this kind of thing happening, and it seemed apparent that this was about the last place in the world he wanted to be. The general vibe he projected was one of urgency—"Let's get this done and move on." I couldn't blame him. I felt much the same way.

Jaime kept trying to bring up lighter topics in an effort to sunny up my mood, but I was dour and angry and excited and in no way interested in cheering up. It didn't help that the conveyor belt started a moment later, and I had to stand there in anticipation of Cooper joining the luggage. We waited and waited. Then finally a couple of bags came out. Then more bags. Then more waiting. And at long last, way at the end of everything, Cooper's crate came sliding out.

And there he was, all the glory that was Cooper. As I got closer, I realized that, from head to toe, he was covered in his own pee and poop. His food and water were scattered all over the floor of his crate. His blankets were caked in filth. My first reaction was to gasp.

He wriggled and bounded inside his crate. And when I let him out, matted and smelly as he was, he just stood there, happy as could be. I took him in my arms and hugged him, that foul smell sticking to me. I didn't care. None of it mattered.

"Cooper, thank God!"

Jaime, Henry, and the airline staff gave us a few moments to get reacquainted before the final paperwork could begin.

Dr. Henry reminded me that Cooper would have to remain in quarantine for thirty days. He explained that he would visit randomly to check up on us. Cooper wouldn't be able to leave the compound or have any interaction with the other animals on the property. I assured Dr. Henry that I understood and that all of this would be fine. But as far as I was concerned, for the duration of Cooper's stay on this island, there would never be anything else that would impede his freedom.

And then we were off. We loaded Cooper and his filthy crate into Jaime's car, and we were on our way home.

CHAPTER SEVEN

The Drugs Take Hold

Now Cooper and I were together again, I knew that my life on the island was never going to go back exactly to the way it was before his arrival, but I had no idea how complicated the situation would become. After bathing him thoroughly, my first order of business was to let him run around the expansive yard for a while and get him acquainted with life in the compound. We still had a couple of days left before the new semester began, and I planned to spend as much of that time as possible with Cooper.

"Gimme that stick." I giggled as we played his favorite tug-of-war game with a branch from the yard. When I finally got control of it, I fired the slobbering thing into the yard to the left of the house. It twirled against the backdrop of the deep-blue island sky before dropping into the ruddy grass beneath an avocado tree.

Rather than perform his end of the fetch routine, Cooper plopped down in the shade of that tree and started to gnaw on the stick.

I looked at him and smiled.

His shoulders rippled as he repositioned the stick with his paws and got to work on the bark with his back teeth.

"Okay. Have it your way." I went to him and sat down with my back against the avocado tree. I set my hand between his busy shoulders and scratched him lightly.

He huffed with contentment.

I sighed into the peace of the moment. A soft breeze blew the salt air from the Caribbean as the shadows of the tree caressed my sun-warmed skin. Cooper's fur was thick and clean and warm. I could have just set my head down right there and fallen asleep on his back. Suddenly he looked back at me, his stick-slobbery lips pulling back into a smile. I beamed back at him, so relieved to have my best friend at my side again.

"We've been through a lot, haven't we, Coopie?"

He gave a throaty grunt and went back to his stick.

Here we would live, Cooper and I. When I paused to think about it, the whole thing just felt so unlikely. When I first met my dog, he had been this adorable puppy without a care in the world, and I had been a part-time waitress and aspiring vet in Blacksburg, VA. Now the two of us lived on a tropical island—an unquestionable paradise, even with my demanding studies and his epilepsy with which to contend.

"We're getting it done, though, aren't we?"

The next breeze brought with it the sense that everything was going to be okay here—or anywhere, for that matter—as long as we were together.

• • •

The first weekend after classes had started up again, my friends and I were engaged in a perfect day at the beach. Everyone was hanging out, enjoying some cocktails and sunshine, drinking in the music and wading in the water. Cooper was also doing many of those things, except his configuration was more like wading through the music and drinking the water. With so many other dogs out there to play with, he was having a grand old time bounding around off leash. Together, he and his new friends dug holes into the beach, peed on everything that smelled like it could use a good marking, and attacked every wave that dared face them.

After a while, we drifted the party over to Inon's. Cooper and I set up at the bar running along the outside of the straw hut. There, Inon himself, the thoroughly stoned caricature of a Rastafarian, slung the drinks to my friends and me. Next to the bar glistened a murky salt pond. It was more of a marsh, really, complete with the promise of quicksand and the aggressive outhouse stench. My friends and I were having such a good time that I took my eye off Cooper.

"Where's Cooper?" I said upon looking down to find he was no longer smiling up from his usual spot at my feet.

On cue, there emerged from the salt pond a creature that at first looked a dead ringer to "the Thing" before all the gross water and sand sloughed off him and he was just a pretty dog with a matted, rancid coat. Not even in his shit-smeared crate at the St. Kitts airport had he ever smelled so terrible. It was so bad, I knew I had to some-how wash him off before I could even let him back in my house to bathe him. The only choice was to lead him into the ocean to cleanse him as best I could. He drank as much as he let me splash over his face and head.

Three days later, he started seizing. These were alarm-ing seizures because they were well ahead of his usual schedule. This would be my first harrowing lesson in the pitfalls of how certain drugs interact with the patient's environment. For a while back in Pittsburgh, Cooper had found himself on the maximum dose of phenobarbital, which Dr. Donaldson had at some point decided was probably best to avoid. So she had switched him to a com-bination of the phenobarbital and potassium bromide, another anticonvulsant that would be gentler on his liver while also sparing him the desire to drink whole lakes of water every day. What Dr. Donaldson neglected to tell me—and who could blame her, since she lived nowhere near an ocean?—was that potassium bromide and salt water simply do not mix. So that's how I learned the hard way not to let a dog on KBR drink his way through half of the Caribbean. Cooper's early seizures were my fault, and it was all because I didn't know about an adverse drug interaction. In some ways, that was my first indelible les-son as a veterinarian, taught to me by my faithful pup. I would never forget it.

Then there was the Diazepam, which is commonly prescribed to treat alcohol withdrawal, anxiety disorders, and muscle spasms. Mostly, it'll just chill you the hell out. Its widely marketed name is Valium. I would give it to Cooper immediately after he had a particularly bad seizure, and that would help even him out. Because, yes, it *is* a controlled substance. This meant that the neurologist who prescribed it to Cooper also had to write a note that I could show to any pharmacist, customs agent, or other authority particularly interested in drug-trafficking patterns on Caribbean islands, assuring them that I was not in fact a drug dealer or addict. Cooper was, after all, on an awful lot of diazepam, and whenever he needed it, he would need a lot of it, so we would go through it like water. There was so much of it coming my way that I would've raised more than a few red flags if not for those notes from the neurologist.

I learned—through textbooks and Cooper himself—that the drug is supposed to settle down brainwave activity, which in turn stops a pattern of seizures as soon as they start. So I didn't have him on the stuff all the time. He just got one of the little tablets immediately after he had any seizures that lasted longer than thirty seconds. Feeding him the things was never all that difficult, because dogs tend to be seriously food driven after a seizure, so he would usually just gobble it ravenously from my hand.

At the time, Cooper's drug regimen had felt pretty hefty. Over the years to come, I would learn that animals can find themselves staggering into a long list of prescriptions related to various ailments. It's really just a matter of how dedicated their people are to ensuring a high quality of life. In my starry-eyed days of vet school, though, I felt a little uncomfortable handling all the diazepam and phenobarbital I would pick up at the school pharmacy each week, along with the potassium bromide that my parents would have to FedEx me from the States twice monthly because it had to be compounded at a special pharmacy we didn't have on the island.

This seemingly hardcore but actually quite light drug cocktail kept Cooper pretty stable over the weeks and months and semesters to come. As long as I kept him from gulping down any oceans, the rebalanced dosage of phenobarbital and potassium bromide kept his seizures at bay for months at a time. Usually the period between seizures stretched to a couple of months, but once we even went as long as eight months. For a while during that time, I allowed myself to believe that he had somehow gotten over the problem. That first seizure after the long period of health was particularly devastating. But when it was over, I consoled myself with the notion that, overall, they were becoming fewer and farther between.

Even the seizures he did have, I learned to manage in better and better ways. The diazepam tablets would chill him out and make him comfortable even after the worst of them. Cooper was undeniably content during our time on the island. Against all odds, he wasn't just surviving but thriving his way through a rewarding, surprisingly healthy life.

He clearly loved everything about his sunny new surroundings as well. The nice thing about living in a Caribbean-style compound—apart from the obvious benefits of living in a tropical paradise—was that the anti-burglary walls and electric entry gate made it possible to just let Cooper barrel out of the house sans leash. Unlike back home, where he would always have to either wait for me to take him on a walk around the neighborhood or deal with being tied to a tree or a stake, here he had the run of the place. He spent huge swaths of every day just roaming around the considerable grounds of the compound. As long as I kept an eye on the gate whenever someone was coming or going in a car, I never had to worry about him slipping out to explore unsupervised.

Plus, he wasn't the only dog. There was Spike, my landlord's dog. Like some Chows, Spike was somewhat territorial. "Somewhat" is maybe putting it kindly in Spike's case. Little guy was aptly named. He was downright savage to anyone who came into his portion of the yard, in truth. If he didn't know you, he would eat you alive. Fortunately, he was much kinder once you got to know him, and he was always plenty cool with Cooper.

Spike's daughter, the equally aptly named Blossom, was cute and sweet where her father was a curmudgeon. Things did get a little backwoods between them one spring, when father and daughter got together for some action on the front porch. Not many dog owners know this, but sometimes when dogs have sex, they get stuck. This is in part due to the gripping nature of the male dog's penis. That happened to Spike and Blossom. They got tied one evening around midnight, and Blossom was just screaming in pain. I'll never forget that sound, as not only was it genuinely bone-chilling, but it woke Cooper and me—and as it turned out, Jen—from a deep sleep as well.

The three of us sprang from our beds and ran to the front porch, where we found the poor pooches in a tangle of pain.

"What do we do?" I asked Jen. I knew the answer already, but watching two loveable dogs in such an agonizing situation made my desperation rise. My heart pounded, and my eyes began to water.

"There's nothing we can do," Jen said in a voice just above a whisper.

So we had to stand there and watch helplessly as the dogs wound themselves out of their torture. Intervening would have meant getting bit by one or the other—or worse, a tear for one of the dogs. There was nothing we could do to help them come unstuck. It was as though they were glued together, and the only solvent was time. Uncomfortable, uncomfortable time.

Cooper looked agitated. He paced back and forth on the porch, grumbling and looking like he wanted to intervene somehow, and yet instinctually knowing that he couldn't. Jen and I took turns gaping at the ugliness and walking away, tugging at our hair from the frustration.

Eventually father and daughter parted, and I could breathe again.

Shortly after, it became clear that Blossom was pregnant with her father's offspring. Weird and disturbing though this was, soon the compound was crawling with adorable Chow puppies.

Cooper became something of a foster dad to a few of them, while Jake—my roommate Jen's Rhodesian Ridgeback—took a couple others under his paw. Jake wasn't much more than a puppy himself. He was a rescue, which was immediately evident by the scar that ran the length of his back. The official story was that he had gotten that scar after being thrown over a fence and snagging himself on the way down. The likely truth was much more gruesome. Ridgebacks have this lion-like mane along their spines, a line of fur that runs in a direction counter to the rest of their coats. There are monstrous people in this world who value the look of that mane to the point that they cut it off the still-living dog's back. There are many practices in the world of household pet breeding that make me cringe, but this one is among the most disgusting. So Jake had that one unimaginably terrible moment from his past. Otherwise, he was a perfectly happy and handsome young dog. He and Cooper were roughly the same age and temperament, and were best buds as a result.

Most veterinary programs are four years of eight total semesters. They often conduct these semesters in five-month stretches before giving the student six weeks or so off prior to the next semester. Ross, being an accelerated program, was different. It scattered its semesters in three-month increments with only two or three weeks of break in between. Obviously, this meant that the breaks were more frequent, but offered a narrower window to do things like travel back home. Making that trip was pretty costly, too, averaging somewhere in the $1,300 to $1,500 range. As a result, most of the non-wealthy students at Ross rarely returned to the States to visit family.

By December of my second year, Cooper and I had spent all our breaks together on the island, but I found myself getting a bit homesick. I had thought for a long while that I would probably suffer through it for the duration of the program, but Cooper was doing really well on his medications, and his seizures were more under control. Plus, as it happened, because of Cooper's predictable seizure schedule, it looked like I would be able to take a two-week trip home for Christmas and make it back before his next attack. So I reached deep into my checking account, told myself I would be able to live on the cheap for the rest of my time on the island, and booked a flight.

Now all I needed to do was find someone I could trust to watch Cooper for the next two weeks. That's where a classmate named Shannon came in.

"You sure you've got this?" I said after we had gone over Cooper's daily feeding and medication regimen a third time.

I knew I didn't really have to ask, because Shannon was one of the smartest and most organized people in my class. As if sensing that I was feeling a little overbearing on the subject, Shannon broke into one of those effortlessly pretty smiles that always seem to come naturally to tall, thin women with glasses, short blond hair, and fair, freckled complexions. "It's no problem. I'll be handling more animals than this when I'm a vet someday."

I laughed at the realization that I was asking a future veterinarian—and a bright one, at that—whether she could handle taking care of a dog's medications. But then I felt another one of those parental moments of dread. I took a step back and noticed just how many animals were running around Shannon's apartment. There was a small pack of dogs, and several cats lounging here and there. There were maybe eight animals in all, not counting Cooper, who had joined the pack of dogs wandering and wrestling around the house.

"Yeah, but how many pets do you have here anyway?" I asked with a scrunched nose.

Shannon furrowed her brow. "I'll have ten here at home once everybody's done bringing them over. One more cat's coming after Cooper. Then that's it." She smiled again. "Plus there's another four cats and six dogs I'll be checking in on at other apartments."

My eyes went wide. "So you're watching, what? Like, *twenty* pets? For two weeks?"

She shrugged. "Great practice for running a clinic."

The thought worried me, but I couldn't deny how right she was. And there was something about Shannon anyway—a quiet confidence I couldn't quite place. I could see she would be fine with Cooper, no matter what his circumstances might bring.

"I'll be in touch every day."

"Don't worry about it." She batted her hand casually. "It's not a problem. I've got your—" she paused to smile at the papers I had given her—"really *thorough* notes. It's a full schedule, but we're on break. I can't think of anything I'd rather do than surround myself with everyone's pets."

I sighed myself calm. "Okay. You're right. I won't bother you too much. I'm still going to email though, okay?"

"And I'll reply quickly. I plan to send everyone an update every night."

That put me at ease. So did the sight of Cooper having so much fun in his new environment with his new dog friends that he hardly even noticed how I was getting ready to leave.

"Okay, Coop," I called out. "I'm gonna go."

He just kept bounding around with his friends.

"Okay then," I said, a little louder now.

A pretty Golden squared off with him in a game of tug-of-war over a rope toy. At the sound of my voice, Cooper cast me a sidelong glance, but didn't let go of the rope. Shannon and I laughed. Then, tearing up a little, I went over to my best friend, squatted down, and gave him a hug as he kept up with his game.

"I love you," I said. "I'll be right back."

It was a long flight home. My anticipation of seeing my family for the first time in a year warred with my sorrow about having to part with Cooper. I kept telling myself that he was in good hands—and I knew completely that it was true. It was still difficult to leave my baby behind.

· · ·

For my two weeks back home, I felt lighter than I could ever remember feeling. Taking on vet school and a dog with a demanding schedule of care was more of a stress load than I had realized. That relatively short stay with family and old friends was about as fulfilling as anything I had ever experienced. The nightly emails from Shannon kept me uplifted as well. Cooper had been enjoying himself immensely in my friend's temporary domestic menagerie.

Then, two days before I was to return, the email from Shannon was of the kind I had been dreading in the back of my mind.

"Cooper had a bad seizure this morning," she wrote. "He had a few of them right in a row, actually. I gave him the diazepam, but it didn't make a difference. I tried to wait it out, but he had another bad seizure and wound up aspirating. I had to take him to the ER clinic. He's been there for the rest of the day today. I tried calling, but the lines weren't working, so I'll have to try again later. He's stable right now, but we should talk about his condition."

Immediately I tried calling in to Shannon using one of those prepaid calling cards that were so essential back in those days. Of course after a few rings, I heard only the signal that said the lines were still down at St. Kitts. Calling that island was always such an expensive and frustrating thing. Given how essential this particular call felt, I was ready to just about break down the walls of my basement bedroom. I logged on to AOL Instant Messenger in the hopes of catching Shannon, but she was away—no doubt tending to the needs of the other twenty animals under her care.

Without any news available, I spent a sleepless night worrying about just how bad Cooper's latest bout of seizures had been, and what had come of this aspiration situation.

Cooper's latest bout of seizures and the aspiration situation had been particularly awful, as it turned out. The next day, Shannon and I finally managed to connect over the phone.

"He's stable then?" I pleaded.

It seemed a long while before she answered. "He is. But that's not really the concern right now."

Not until later would I realize that I had been clenching my teeth hard enough to give myself a lasting headache. I didn't know how to reply.

"Katti, I'm really sorry," Shannon said. From her tone, I felt certain that she was about to tell me my dog had passed away. "They told me he has aspiration pneumonia. They have him on oxygen, which I guess is kind of hard to come by on an island. The drugs are supposedly really expensive too."

"But he's going to be okay, right?" I said, the tears falling over my cheeks.

Another long silence followed. I thought I heard a sniffle from Shannon, and it just about ripped my heart in half. "Just hurry back, okay? If you can move your flight up, you might want to."

"Shannon, I—"

"They're just not sure he's going to make it," she cut in, and now I could hear that she was crying.

My heart sank. A wave of frantic anxiety came over me. I felt sick to my stomach. I heard myself thanking Shannon and telling her it wasn't her fault, but already my mind was racing ahead to figure out just how I could get back to the island as soon as possible. I had done enough research into the flights over the years that I knew my options were limited. My scheduled flight would leave in just a bit less than twenty-four hours, but there was another that I could board in six hours or so. I made the call to the airline to find out how much it would cost to switch, even though I knew it wouldn't be anywhere near within reach.

It was painful to hear how right I was. I just wanted to get back. Just wanted to be in St. Kitts at that ER clinic, standing next to my poor dog as he breathed his forced oxygen and fought to survive. For the first time since his grim diagnosis, I felt that harrowing, dark feeling that he would die. Shannon had sounded so resigned, so regretful. Part of me thought that if I was there with Cooper, maybe it would give him that last bit of encouragement he needed to overcome. The more logical part of me knew that the best I could do was comfort him as a friend as he passed.

I was a wreck that day. My hands were shaking so badly, I found it difficult to pack. The sleep that took me that night only did so because I was too emotionally and physically exhausted to fight it. The morning would bring the sweet hope of a flight, but even that seemed like an obstacle, given that I would be in the air a full nine hours and in airports another three or four on top of that.

There's not much I remember about that trip back. It was just such a cloud of dread and heartbreak. I wanted badly for the journey to be over, but at the same time, I knew what awaited me. For Cooper's sake, I yearned to be there. For my own ailing heart, the prospect of watching my dog die was more than I could bear.

Timi, my best friend on the island, proved saintly in that moment she arrived to pick me up at the airport. I was blanketed by the grease a girl picks up in the recycled air of an airplane, hot-sweating from the humid heat, and cold-sweating from the dread, and there Timi sat idling in her white Hyundai Elantra, a sympathetic gaze shining my way. I slid my huge suitcase into the backseat, then heard the pop of a bottle cap as soon as I sat down in the weirdly left-hand passenger side.

"You look like you could use this," Timi said, handing me an ice-cold beer.

I had never been so thrilled to remember how relaxed St. Kitts was about its drinking and driving laws. Open containers were no problem, and this particular open container was a miracle for me. Even as I took my first swig, I noticed out the corner of my eye how Timi had stuck two cigarettes in her lips and was lighting them simultaneously. The moment I set my beer back into the cup holder, she was handing me a smoke.

"This, too."

I was nothing more than a social smoker—usually the occasional cig while drunk—but I accepted it gratefully. The look I gave Timi as I took a long drag was one of awe. There are no other women on this planet quite like her. Originally from Delaware, she was, and is, the most fun, energetic, delightfully loud person I have ever met. She was also improbably loyal. Everyone loved her.

There was any number of things she could have said to me in that moment. She could have consoled me. Could have said she was sorry. Could have pretended at optimism and told me that Cooper would pull through, even though everyone seemed to think it was all over. But instead, she did what only Timi could do: she said the absolute perfect thing. She reached her well-tanned left hand to the stick, threw the car into drive, and said, "Let's go." Then she rolled the windows down, her light brown, blond-streaked hair fluttering in the wind as we sped as fast as the Elantra and the potholed roads would allow. Timi was short like me, and she was cute and funny. Maybe it was the beer and the smoke, but more likely it was the very Timi-ness of my friend. Whatever the case, I felt myself calming down for the first time since learning the news.

We made it to the hospital in record time. Cooper had been transferred to the ICU, and he looked every bit as bad as I feared. He was ashen, his breathing labored, his neck stretched out and his eyes shut tight as if every breath were a strain. They had outfitted him with a bilateral nasal cannula, a set of transparent tubes that ran up his nose deeply enough to pass through the sinuses beside his eyes. The whole thing was held in place by a set of straps that clasped behind his head. I felt sure he wasn't enjoying anything about it. Just the look of him confirmed it. It was almost as if he was sedated, even though I knew he wasn't. I set my quivering hand on his quivering shoulder and hoped desperately that I would get to see those big brown eyes again.

Once I had seen enough, I found myself wandering the small hospital in search of someone who could give me some answers. Of all people, I found Dr. Morrison, my neurology professor who also happened to be entirely dreamy. He had that South African accent of his, and the long, wavy, blondish hair he kept pulled back in a ponytail. There were those small, wire-rimmed glasses, that nice smile, and the adorably charming personality. He had an effortlessly cool, hippy on a surfboard vibe about him. Many of the girls at the vet school had a crush on him, and most of the guys loved him too because he was just about as cool and down to earth as a human being could be. When I saw him, I couldn't decide whether his beauty would make it easier or harder to hear what seemed certain to be bad news.

He was in the clinic attached to the hospital. It was a comically small place with a single storm door for its only entry and absolutely no windows. More of a bomb shelter, really, if you can imagine a bomb shelter dumb enough to exist above ground. Through the door was a small, dreary waiting room with two chairs, and beyond the reception desk was the lone exam room. The receptionist doubled as the only technician. She was the only employee, really, as the vets all technically fell under the employ of the vet school itself.

The clinic lacked the technological bells and whistles Cooper had gotten so familiar with at all the hospitals and clinics back home, but the people were always kind and energetic in finding solutions to keep him healthy and happy. A number of teaching rooms surrounded the place, where students practiced the arts of surgery, applying bandages, and so on. These rooms assembled into an area that bled into the main hospital.

Dr. Morrison was just finishing up his rounds in that little concrete box of a clinic when I happened upon him. The handsome doctor nodded when he saw me. "You made it."

"I feel so terrible that I wasn't here for him," I said. "Is he… is he going to be—"

"It's touch and go," Dr. Morrison said softly.

I took a deep, shuddering breath. "How did…?"

"It looks like he was on too much potassium bromide." The handsome doctor checked his clipboard. "Looks like it was the maximum dose."

"So the potassium bromide—"

"Over time, it can cause megaesophagus. In Cooper's case, he has suffered irreversible loss of muscle in his esophagus, which makes him prone to aspiration pneumonia."

The way he looked at me, it was as if he expected me to know everything there was to know about megaesophagus. Whether I hadn't learned about it yet in class or was too flustered to recall, I'm not sure, but I gave him a blank look.

"It's like he has a big, floppy bag in his neck," he said. "Food just sits there without being able to go down into his stomach."

"So that's what caused his pneumonia?"

He nodded. Then he started to ramble on about the whys before he put on his professor face and slowed it down for me. "There's really nothing you could have done. It wasn't your fault. His seizures were so severe; I wasn't surprised to find that we were pushing the limits on his dosage. I just wish we had realized this in time."

I gave a sorrowful nod.

"When he wakes—" and he paused for a moment as if to make sure I heard his certainty about Cooper's waking— "we're going to scale him back on his current meds and switch him to Felbamate or Gabapentin." He made a note on his clipboard. "They're anticonvulsants too. The Gabapentin might make him a little loopy, but the side effects are otherwise minimal. The Felbamate is expensive and a little tough to come by on the island, but we can work it out. It should all make him more comfortable while still helping regulate his seizures without having an effect on his esophagus."

I thanked Dr. Morrison and went back to check on my best friend. As I approached him, it dawned on me that I'd been compulsively biting my lip since my arrival on the island. This latest bite drew a trace of blood. It tasted metallic and strangely sweet, matching the vision of ever-sweet Cooper lying there in that stainless steel cage, hooked up to all those machines. I let out a soft sigh as I reached out and placed my hand on the side of his neck. When I laced my fingers into his fur, he seemed to stir. Then his eyes fluttered halfway open and sent my heart soaring.

"Oh, Cooper."

At the sound of my voice, he jolted and tried to sit up, but I soothed him back down with my hand.

"Rest, sweet boy," I said. "You're going to get through this. And I swear I'm never leaving you behind again."

For the rest of his life, I kept true to that vow. Sure, I'd go out from time to time and settle him in with a friend or family or kennel for a night or even a weekend, but I made sure that I never again needed a plane to get to my best friend when he needed me.

"Sounds like we're switching you onto some new

drugs," I said. "Hopefully, they don't feel too much like a party." I chuckled at the thought of Cooper smile-drooling through a loopy little high. It was a funny picture, but I knew I wasn't going to let it happen. My goal wasn't to just keep Cooper alive, after all. I wanted him to have a high quality of life.

Cooper huffed in a distressed way, almost as if questioning how much this was all going to cost me.

"Don't you worry," I told him. "It's like Dr. Morrison said. We'll work it out."

It turned out that Cooper was right. The Felbamate and Gabapentin were crazy expensive, as was his latest turn in the hospital. Out of all the line items on his bill, the oxygen was by far the most costly. From the outside looking in, it might seem strange to think that a huge component of the air we breathe would be so very expensive, but then it occurred to me that it wasn't as if they could manufacture the stuff on the island. They just didn't have the facilities. Plus, compressed oxygen is highly flammable, which makes it difficult to transport. Likely they had to ship it by boat, since getting it on a plane would reside somewhere between impossible and insane. This meant oxygen was in short supply on St. Kitts, which in turn meant that the expense was equally impossible and insane.

By then, it didn't matter. I had quit caring about what managing Cooper's health was costing me. Anyone who has had a loved one endure a long-term medical crisis and the associated expense would agree that there always comes a point when the money doesn't matter anymore.

Usually it's right at the start, but sometimes the sticker shock sticks around for a week or two. But always—always—you reach that plateau where you don't even blink at all the zeros lining up on the medical bills. I'd already spent thousands of dollars to keep my dear friend happy and as healthy as his condition would allow; what was a few thousand more?

Apart from the expense, the problem with Gabapentin in particular is that for Cooper, it behaved almost like an upper. This little pill sent him to crazy town. Most dogs don't have this particular side effect, but Cooper went absolutely sideways. Not long after his release from the hospital, I came into the parking lot at the compound and found Cooper gnawing on the bumper of my car. If you've had a dog for any stretch of time, it's pretty easy to prepare yourself to find him doing just about any crazy-dog thing you can think of, but to see Cooper mistaking a 3,000-pound automobile for a chew toy covered in peanut butter—well, that was a different level of bananas entirely. Dr. Morrison had hinted at a bit of loopiness, but my dog was completely stoned. He was constantly hungry, and often didn't seem entirely himself. With all the skittishness and wild behavior, I was soon convinced that we needed a different solution. Plus, it seemed as if the stuff fell short of regulating his seizures anyway.

So we shifted him off the sparkle pills and onto a fuller run of Felbamate, which was every bit as expensive and difficult to acquire as Dr. Morrison had warned. He spent a month or two on this drug before we realized that it wasn't helping his seizures either.

"We'll put him back on some of the potassium bromide." Dr. Morrison smiled as he scratched Cooper behind the ears. "It's generally better at controlling seizures anyway, but I'm starting to think maybe our boy here has been on it so long that it's the only thing that will really work for him."

As he leaned into the scratch, Cooper gave a look like all the vet school girls so regularly shined on Dr. Morrison.

"We'll rebalance his dosage of Phenobarbital, potassium bromide, and Gabapentin to relieve his liver a little and let us cut down on the side effects. And it should still normalize his seizures, just like you've been used to. It might even improve things from before his incident."

With the plan in mind and the new prescriptions in hand, Cooper and I bounded out of the bomb shelter. That was how we arrived at a new configuration of the small cocktail of pills that helped Cooper enjoy himself 99% of the days of his life. Almost immediately, they brought him back to the balance and comfort we were looking for, so we kept him on those dosages for the time. He really kind of loved it, mostly because I would give him his pills stuffed inside little meatballs. I did this in part because he adored them and in part because the meatball's spherical shape meant it could roll down his suddenly looser esophagus without getting stuck.

That wasn't the only part of his care that changed because he now carried a floppy little food-catcher around in his throat. His condition meant that he couldn't eat straight kibble anymore. That would've required too much muscle action. So I had to soak his food in water and mash it into a slurry to make it easier to process and swallow. On top of that, he couldn't eat on all fours like most dogs because gravity would pull his freshly chomped meals down into his new built-in danger bag. So I had to change the gravitational pull by feeding him upright. This meant setting Cooper's bowl on the counter and holding him in a hind-leg standing position while he mowed down on his dinner. So picture a hundred-pound girl standing behind a hundred-pound dog, straining to prop him up on the counter so he could eat like some kind of furry, floppy-jowled aristocrat. It was high class all the way in our kitchen.

Usually the program worked, but sometimes he would still retch up some of his food and inhale it from the pocket in his neck. That would cause him to aspirate, and I'd have to take him back to the hospital. It didn't happen often, and he was always so happy and healthy in the in-between. But that was just problem number two of what would basically become about ten problems.

Problem number three was his tendency to wander. It wasn't the first and wouldn't be the last time I would have to face problem number three, but it would be one of the strangest. Our little compound was accessed by a wide, metal gate that slid open automatically at the touch of a button. This was fine with me, as it kept me and my roommate feeling safer. At the same time, the thing about high security is that it can sometimes trick you into a false sense of total security. Cooper loved that gate and fence because it meant he would never have to go with a leash or chain while at home. As long as I was around to check on him from time to time, he could just run out the door and tool around the big yard to his heart's content.

The problem with that automatic gate is that it closed pretty slowly. If Cooper had a mind to bail, he could have just tailed out of there after a car came through. I'd kept a wary eye on the gate for as long as we had been living on the island and had even managed to train Cooper into something of a reverence for the thing. He seemed to know that it was against the rules to approach it whenever it was open, in any case.

At least that's what I thought. One night, fairly late, the gate never managed to close for whatever reason, and when I went into the back yard, I couldn't find Cooper. Most of the time, it was almost a given that he would be lying in ecstasy under the avocado tree, but no, he wasn't there.

Panicking, I ran to my landlord's house, the one next to mine. Michael Gresseau shared his home with his well-tanned, seventy-year-old mother, who was the one to answer the door. Mrs. Gresseau was shorter, stocky, and possessed of an island accent so thick that I couldn't understand half the things she said to me at any given time. Since she rarely looked at me with anything kinder than abject suspicion, I half-suspected she was doing it on purpose. The elder Gresseau almost always wore nightgowns. The one she wore to the door that day was off-white and drapey and wreathed with a floral print from neck to considerable breast. She gave me the tired eye before turning to shout for her son. I liked her, even if the feeling wasn't mutual. On any other occasion, I might have tried to ingratiate myself, but I was too busy fretting about Cooper to make small talk while we waited for my landlord.

Michael arrived a few seconds later. He was maybe six feet tall but looked much taller because he was skinny as a board. He had dark hair and a nice smile and would have been genuinely attractive if not for the waifishness one might normally associate with hard drug use. He wasn't on drugs as far as I knew. More likely, he just needed to eat a few more sandwiches.

"Yes?"

Just like everyone born and raised on the island, the younger Gresseau was a genuinely kind man. Unlike most everyone else born and raised on the island, he was awkward and of few words—one of those guys who was nice and even engaging if you got him talking, but getting him talking took about as much back-rending effort as starting an old lawnmower.

"The door is open," I said with dramatic flair.

Michael looked at the swinging screen door he held open with his hand, then gave a quick glance back at his disapproving mother.

"No, the gate," I said. "The front gate. It's wide open."

At first, I think he and Mrs. Gresseau mistook my anxiousness for fear that the longer the gate stayed open, the sooner the raping and pillaging hordes would notice and break through. Mrs. Gresseau's expression melted into incredulity as her son sighed and nodded.

"Cooper's missing," I explained. "I think he must have wandered out when the gate didn't close."

Now I had Michael's attention. As a kind man and a dog owner himself, he could clearly understand how this would be distressing. So he hopped back into the relative darkness of the house and returned with his shoes, a floppy pair of sneakers so old and dirty that they left streaks of black soot on his fingers as he put them on.

Together with my pasty beanpole of a landlord, I entered the island night in search of my missing friend. Most of St. Kitts was quite lovely and safe, but a few neighborhoods—and in particular, some of the ones surrounding the compound in which I lived—were more than a little shady. My landlord's body language suggested he had that thought in mind as we wandered the streets calling for Cooper. I was so worried as to be completely oblivious.

At the end of the block, we passed OOJJ's gas station, closed for the night, its Bob Marley mercifully silent. If I'd had to listen to even one measure of "Three Little Birds" while panic-searching for Cooper, I might have lost it. We turned the corner into something of a ghetto, which caused Mr. Gresseau to slow down some and his eyes to widen into protective mode.

"Cooper!" I kept hollering.

Michael didn't appear to enjoy the attention all the yelling was causing, but he eventually joined in as well. Like I said, he was kind.

"Cooper!" he yelled in his fetching accent.

We wandered past broken-down cars propped up on blocks, cinderblock homes with neither doors nor windows, and scrap metal stacked up in yards. Many of the houses had goats tied to stakes out front, the scrawny little waifs chewing cartoonishly on the sparse grass poking up through the debris. All the while, Mr. Gresseau and I yelled for Cooper, drawing the eye of anyone still up.

"Cooper, do you want your pills?" I called out.

Mr. Gresseau bent his wiry frame into a wince.

"Cooper, do you want your pills?" Every time I said it, I pictured him peeling out of some strand of mango trees, tongue flopping in excitement. Mention of his pills always sent him running my way because he was so in love with those meatballs.

"Cooper, do you want—"

I felt my landlord's hand on my forearm. I looked up at him, and he was white as a sheet, almost trembling neon in the dark night.

"You really shouldn't yell that out here," he said in a voice just above a whisper.

I paused to gather myself and assess my surroundings. Two young men in the house to our left were giving us the stink-eye as they kicked back in rickety lawn chairs set up on their porch. Next door, an angry looking gentleman with a bandana tied around his arm kept his gaze trained on us hungrily. It suddenly occurred to me what I was doing.

"If the drug lords hear you yelling that…" my landlord said, not bothering to finish.

I nodded. Then together we shuffled as quickly as possible to the other end of the block. From that point forward, it would be just, "Cooper, come," with no mention of delicious drugs.

By sheer luck, it turned out that Dr. Morrison was out for a midnight ride when he came across Cooper. Maybe my friend had grown fond of my handsome professor, or maybe he just missed visiting the clinic on the regular since it had been an uncommonly long time since our last visit. Something drew him to the neighborhood surrounding Ross, and there he happened upon the best possible person not named Katti to find him.

"I guess he just needed a full-moon stroll," Dr. Morrison said with that easy smile.

As I squatted to give Cooper one of those embraces that says, "I'm so glad to see you, but don't ever do that again," I took a nervous look over my shoulder and noticed that the moon was indeed full. It was a good thing, because street lighting on the island wasn't particularly thorough or reliable, so without that light, we might not have been able to see our way through the unwelcoming places we had wandered that night.

"Thank you so much, Dr. Morrison." I stood, swooning into his eyes.

"Don't mention it," he said. "I didn't find him. He found me."

I knew exactly how my professor felt. Cooper's life was occasionally complicated, and more than a few times, I had questioned why the two of us would want to endure so much trouble to stay together. But that was the answer, really. Back when I was a bright-eyed college graduate, I had gone out looking for a puppy, but in many ways, Cooper had found me.

CHAPTER EIGHT

Hurricane Cooper

You'll always remember your first. That's what they say anyway.

For two generations of Gresseau, I suspect that the notion absolutely applies to their first tenants—or at least to their first tenants' dogs. They had found themselves with tenants in the first place because they happened to live in a compound with three houses, and they happened to know Michelle, the woman in charge of finding and securing housing for vet students at Ross.

There had never really been a plan to take in the people and money that would come from renting a house, but fate would make the situation fairly unavoidable for Michael. He had a daughter and a wife from England, both of whom would need to take a long-term leave from the island when his mother-in-law became sick. The plan was for his family to be away for as long as it took.

When that turned into the better part of a year, Michael decided to take Michelle up on her offer.

With three houses inside the fence, he could move himself out of the one he had shared with his family and into one of the other two. His choice was either to live with his mother or to live with his brother, who was a surfer and admittedly more than a bit of a partier. The brother's love of good times was to the point where I hardly ever saw him during my entire stay on the island. The more responsible Michael made the obvious choice to avoid sharing space with his less responsible little brother and instead joined his mother. The house he had vacated would now set up nicely for his very first tenants, Jen and me. And Jake. And Cooper.

We must have seemed quite a handful, but the Gresseau clan always treated us well. Even the elder Gresseau, who had seemed so skeptical of the American girls at first, eventually relaxed enough in our company to smile from time to time when we caught her eye. Mostly, though, she just went about her life as if we weren't there.

One such day happened to be Mother's Day, a holiday Mrs. Gresseau had turned into an opportunity to cook a traditional brunch. Jen and I weren't invited to join, but we could certainly smell all the action wafting from the Gresseau kitchen next door. Being that I was a grad student with a dog whose medical bills were nearly the equivalent of the St. Kitts annual tourism revenues, it had been quite a while since I had enjoyed a proper meal. So to say that the aromas were enough to give me heart palpitations wouldn't be quite enough to explain how deeply emotional it made me. That day, I think I experienced for the first and only time what it was like to have a dog's almost supernatural sense of smell. I could smell every morsel of the ham, the turkey, the eggs, the various potatoes, the candied local fruits, the bread, and on and on. I can't remember ever salivating quite so openly.

I guess everyone else was at church while Mrs. Gresseau was finishing her preparations of what promised to be a giant feast, because I would later learn that she was home alone at the time. Jen and I happened to be taking a study break on the front porch when I spotted the elder Gresseau shuffling out to take a break in the sunshine beaming over the rocking chair she kept beside her front door. Jen had suggested that we step outside, where our proximity to the scent of the mango tree would hopefully drown out the intoxicating promise of all that gloriously home-cooked food. The mangoes were no match.

"What I wouldn't give for just one bite of that turkey," Jen said.

"Some ham and eggs and maybe some toast," I said wistfully.

Jen got up and smiled through a groan. "Why is she torturing us like this?"

I shook my head. "She doesn't even know."

And there the matriarch sat, a casual little scowl on her lips as she rocked through the sunshine and waited.

Cooper was patrolling the yard, I knew, so I called out to him for some company and distraction. In short order, he appeared from around the corner of the Gresseau house and sauntered over. He stayed just long enough for a scratch behind the ears before taking off again in the same direction from where he came.

For a time, I managed to forget about the food by concentrating on the sunshine. Soon, I found myself wondering why it was that not everyone chose to live on a tropical island. If I hadn't been so close to my family back home, I might have considered taking up residence there. It was all just so idyllic. There was very little ugly to this place, and even the ugly to be found seemed to fit perfectly with the beauty all around. The ghettos and drug runners had their places, and it all served in a weird way to harmonize the environment. The sun was warm. The people were kind. Life drifted leisurely. The breezes were soft and sweet.

I didn't even startle when Jen spoke a little louder than expected after the few minutes of silence.

"How many times do you think she's basted that turkey?"

I laughed.

"Do you think she'd let us have a plate if we offered to help?"

Again, I laughed. Mrs. Gresseau had come to tolerate us, but she was generally cold. It seemed as though she had gotten to the point where she didn't mind having us around, but it was clear that she still thought of us as something of a nuisance. Still, the idea of some kind of kitchen-help-for-food exchange did sound inviting, if only for a moment. "Mmm," I said dreamily as I leaned back into the chair.

Oblivious to our wants, Mrs. Gresseau kept rocking on the porch opposite us. She had that porch all dolled up with her crocheted pillows and frilly accents she had made to pass the time. Even from this distance, I could make out the purse-lipped smile she shied at the sunny sky as she leaned back into her chair and settled her bones. I matched the effort on my end. A moment later, I looked back, and she was gone, her chair still rocking from her apparently sudden rise.

Inwardly I shrugged and went back to chilling. That chilling was so deep that I startled straight to my feet when I realized Mrs. Gresseau was silently standing over me. It took only one look to make out how she had managed such silence: She was fuming so hard that it seemed like she was having trouble speaking.

"Your dog is, is, is," she said, stalling out as she searched for the right word. "Your dog is *no good*."

I furrowed my brow. "What do you mean?" I asked, thinking how I had just seen Cooper bounding around happily in the yard. "My dog's fine."

For a moment, Mrs. Gresseau looked like part of her wanted to slap me and the other part wanted to just send me away. "You come and see what he's done."

A chill ran down my spine. Across the yard I followed the hobbling Mrs. Gresseau to the back door of her house. That aroma of a fine feast filled my nostrils. What had been such an inviting scent had become something of a warning—the closer I came to the smell, the closer I came to finding out why Mrs. Gresseau was so furious with Cooper.

Like the front porches of all three houses in the compound, the back patio had a swinging screen door that served as the only barrier between the house and the outside world. The door was still there, closed and undamaged, but somehow Cooper had found his way through. My boy was a smart boy. This would be neither the first nor the last obstacle that he somehow managed to riddle his way around.

Mrs. Gresseau reached the door first and turned back to motion at the scene like a product presenter in some backward, terribly wrong infomercial. It is difficult to describe the carnage all over the table and floor behind her.

Cooper had eaten the entire Mother's Day brunch. That isn't even much of an exaggeration. He had hounded through everything. The ham he had reduced to the bone. The turkey was a mutilated carcass. There was no sign of the eggs. All the potatoes were nosed through, many of them still clinging to Cooper's snout. With the beard of mashed potatoes, he looked like a deranged Santa Claus, all hopped up on holiday feast. All the chairs were lying on their sides, kicked over in Cooper's frantic efforts to get to the smorgasbord that had so recently been set up on the table. Every pot in the room was overturned. There was a smattering of casserole spread from one end of the floor to the other with such calculated grace, I had a hard time believing Cooper hadn't planned for it to look that way.

I stood speechless. The quivering anger and embarrassment spread from my belly to my shoulders before rippling down to my fingertips and making me feel numb everywhere. I wanted to cry—out of sorrow and disappointment and overwhelming contrition—so badly that I couldn't even remember how to scream. I just stood there, shaking with rage at Cooper and desperate sympathy for poor Mrs. Gresseau.

Then the weirdest thing happened. I felt about as awful as I had ever felt about anything. The guilt was crippling. It was a sensation that I hadn't known since I was a young girl, but when it came back to me, it was like an old friend. The situation had become untenable. Nothing could be done. I was in so much trouble that there was no way to explain or apologize or atone in a way that would make the offended party forgive me. So, like a small child might do in that situation, I found myself fighting against the dark feelings with an uncontrollable little laugh. I stifled it as best I could. I really did respect Mrs. Gresseau, and I really did feel terrible. But what could I do? This was like a scolding from my second-grade teacher, or like getting yelled at by my own grandma, something that I couldn't really picture happening in the real world. I didn't want to laugh, but I *had* to laugh.

"What am I supposed to do now?" my landlord's mother seethed. "All this work ruined."

"I'm so sorry," I muttered. "What can I do?"

"Nothing. Just get out."

"I want to pay for this," I said. "Please, just—"

"No," Mrs. Gresseau said flatly. "You have done enough, thank you."

With my slight chuckle now replaced with the fury that belonged to the moment, I chased Cooper across the yard and back into my house, where I slammed the door behind him. The guilt returned when I trotted back and reexamined the wreckage my hurricane of a dog had left. All that work ruined. That was one thing. The other was that such a feast must have cost poor Mrs. Gresseau a relative fortune. Like most people on the island, the Gresseau clan didn't have a ton of disposable income. Losing all this food was a big deal. On the one hand, I wished that she would have let me pay for it. On the other, I felt weirdly relieved to be turned away because the truth was that I didn't have the money to pay for it anyway. I had to take out personal loans just to pay for Cooper's care, let alone get by on a price-gouged tropical island while attending an expensive veterinary school. Even if I could have scraped together the hundreds of dollars this all must have cost, it would have broken me for the rest of the year.

In the end, I couldn't do anything but apologize. Several times over the course of the day, I returned to offer help cleaning up, but Mrs. Gresseau was so angry that she banished me from the house every time. After that day, she went back to refusing to hide how little she liked me.

• • •

Since I was enough of an animal lover to honestly believe that I didn't have enough pets or pet problems already, it was right around that time that I took in a new friend. We already had Jake the Rhodesian Ridgeback and Cooper, destroyer of Mother's Day Brunch, but now I started to feel like the place needed a little more balance. Actually, that's not exactly accurate. The truth was that fate put me and my little furry family in the path of a kitten I couldn't resist.

Timi, Laura, Maryam, and I were out hiking along the sugarcane tracks at the bottom of a volcano one day when we heard her cry out. It was a loud, forceful, and altogether desperate sort of meow, and the moment I heard it, I was powerless to resist. To this day, she still has that crazy-loud meow. I like to think it's because she knows that it was exactly that meow that saved her life. If she hadn't been so loud, I don't think we ever would have found her.

When she called again, we went pawing through the cane stalks and eventually found her there, running straight at us on the sugarcane tracks, meowing like the world's cuddliest fire alarm. I could see that she was upset and anxious, and young enough that it seemed likely she had been separated from her mom somehow.

"Oh my God," I said.

"Oh my God," Timi said.

"Oh my God," Maryam said.

"Oh my *God*," Laura said.

We tended to agree like that.

"Oh no, sweetie," I said to the adorable kitten. "How long have you been out here, little guy?" Then I quickly turned the kitten over and realized my mistake. "Little *girl*, I mean."

She meowed and began licking at my fingers. I wanted so badly to resist the urge rising within me, but she made it difficult.

"Who's going to take this kitten?" The truth was, I had no desire for a cat. I didn't grow up with them and never really thought of myself as anything resembling a cat person. Besides, Cooper was enough for me. But, man, that adorable little face and that roaring meow…

"I don't have room for another cat," Timi said.

"I don't want another kitten," Laura and Maryam said at pretty much the exact same time.

So the three cat people in the crowd decided immediately that one more cat would qualify them as crazy cat ladies.

"If I bring in one more," Laura added, "they'll all start marking everything and the whole house will stink."

We all stood there looking at her as she licked my fingers and purred. She was adorable. Completely loveable. I didn't want her in any way but wound up taking her by default. We couldn't just leave her out there, and there was no such thing as a trustworthy animal rescue on the island. Besides, it didn't take long for me to fall in love with her and become something of a cat person after all.

With my faithful dog back home and unaware of what was about to hit him, I carried my new friend back to the house and started the process of nursing her back to health. I named her Liamuiga, or "Lia" for short, in keeping with the local tradition of naming found animals after a feature of the island of St. Kitts. It happened to be the name of the volcano where we discovered her. At first, I worried about how she and Cooper would get along. My boy was used to having all the attention, after all, so it would be interesting to see how he would deal with competition for my affection.

I was not the least bit surprised when Cooper proved himself to be a spectacular big brother. He would look after Lia often, and would snuggle with her pretty much every chance he got. When she was still a kitten, she would run up to him and attack his legs and playfully bat at his tail. Most dogs would have lashed out in that situation, but Cooper seemed to love it. Maybe it was his easygoing nature, or maybe it was just the drugs, but he was all about getting knocked around by that little cat.

Having another playmate seemed to mellow Cooper even further. Now he had a cat to keep him company in the house and Jake to chase around the yard, play tug with sticks, and wrestle with in the warm sun. Even with his drug regimen and oddball dining routine, in those longer and longer intervals between his seizures, life was truly and completely good.

The drug cocktail had the seizures more or less under control again. Cooper actually made it as long as eight months between seizures during one stretch. But when they did happen, they were still so painful to watch. Whenever a bout came around, I would try to find another way to make him comfortable during and after. A pattern of post-seizure behavior emerged early on for Cooper. No matter how long or severe the seizure, he would always pop up after it was finished and just stalk and pace around the house. He would walk and walk and walk, no matter what I did to calm him down.

"Where are you walking to, Cooper?" I would say. "China?"

Sometimes I swear that if we hadn't been contained in that house or on an island, he might have just kept walking until he did indeed reach the other side of the world. I imagine he would have enjoyed a nice fried rice or Lo Mein.

The problem with this behavior in our St. Kitts home was that the slippery tile floor didn't always agree with him. He would wheel around on the back end of his pacing and slip and fall. Then he would get up again and get back to it. Since this was hard enough to watch on its own, and since he often slipped during his seizures as well, I decided to do something to mitigate the situation.

So I bought these socks. They were knee-highs with treads on the bottom. Because life is sometimes perfect, they happened to have Scooby-Doo on them. It's difficult to keep people socks on a dog's skinny legs, so they would slide down on the regular, but the traction on the bottom did help. His seizures would often last about thirty or forty seconds, and when they were over, I would wait for him to calm down long enough to put the socks on. Then he would pace around on his padded Scoobies until he felt comfortable enough to finally lie down again.

Some dogs have comfort toys or blankets or T-shirts. Cooper had Scooby-Doo socks. And we were fortunate to have them, because the few seizures he had on the island wouldn't be the only occasion they came in handy.

• • •

It was September of 2004, which happened to fall in the middle of a terrible hurricane season that few people remember because of the Katrina, Wilma, and Rita horrors that struck the following year. The weather reports during the short lead-up promised us that Hurricane Ivan wasn't going to be a standard Caribbean blowout. It started out as a raging tropical storm, then sucked up enough of the sea to become a category five hurricane measured at sixty-two miles wide. That happened to be roughly the same diameter as the island of St. Kitts, so wherever it made landfall it would bring abject devastation, and here it was heading straight for us.

Back when I first told my parents that I had decided to attend vet school on a tropical island, I could see them immediately start counting the months until hurricane season was officially over. The three late summers and autumns that I was at Ross, my mom and dad would always nervously ask about the weather. My answer was always the same: that I didn't really follow the weather too closely, and that even if I did, there wouldn't be much time to react because the storms would just form right next to us and be on us in a matter of hours. That never gave them much comfort, but it was the truth. Either way, we'd made it through my first pair of hurricane seasons unscathed, but now the big one loomed.

Being terrified about a storm hitting my home in less than a day and seeing how completely laid back all my neighbors and fellow islanders were about the whole thing made for a funny contrast. A person can get used to anything, I suppose, and when you live in the hurricane belt, that's just one of the pills you have to occasionally swallow. Plus, people on St. Kitts were so chill all the time anyway. I don't think I ever once saw a local move at a pace any faster than a lope. Nobody's ever in a hurry to get anywhere or do anything. Their motto, after all, is "rush slowly." Nobody freaks out about anything, let alone the little things that so many people tend to freak out about in the US. Not that an approaching hurricane was a little thing—and this hurricane in particular was massive—but it was still odd to be fretting internally while, everywhere I looked, everyone was just straight *chilling.*

The only thing that even resembled the kind of gravity a typical American would place on such a situation was when we were called into the auditorium at school to be briefed on the coming storm. The building was on campus on the back side of the hill, which meant it overlooked the ocean. Through the two large bay windows behind the presenters, the sea looked about as picturesque and not-at-all-foreboding as it always did. Still, I could see the seriousness in my professors' eyes, and could feel the tension from my classmates, so I'd be lying if I said I wasn't afraid.

We had already been briefed once on what to do in the event of a hurricane—way back during our first-week orientation. So this was a bit of a refresher course for the thousand or so people in attendance. It was Dr. Hutchison, a nice guy but something of a ball-buster of an anatomy professor, who did most of the talking. He was a taller, thin man with round, wire-rimmed glasses and a brown mustache that didn't exactly match his blonder hair. He was extremely intelligent, one of those brilliant minds in his fifties who has studied his craft so completely that he has moved on to master other little sidepieces of knowledge. In this case, Dr. Hutchison was an expert on tropical weather.

He said many things about storm surge and rainfall, wind speeds and evacuation procedures, but the general message was, "Look, there's not a ton we can do here on this island, so you've just got to pay attention and watch out."

Easy enough advice for the islanders and the professors that had been through this all before. They knew the drill. Given the relative poverty and the few transportation options available to them, they had experienced full lives where it was virtually impossible to get off the island in the lead-up to these kinds of crises. So people just became accustomed to battening down the hatches and riding out the squalls.

For the uninitiated among us, the message was terrifying. What made it worse was how little notice this massive hurricane was giving us. In the US, we've grown accustomed to watching storm trackers for days or even a full week at a time before a storm ever makes landfall. But the Caribbean is where storms are born and bred, so there is always the threat of getting crawled over by these baby hurricanes without warning. They're usually quite large babies, too, since hurricanes thrive on warm, open water, and there's no shortage of that in the region occupied by St. Kitts.

The next worst component of the situation was telling my parents. The AOL chat might have lacked the facial expression and tonality so essential to proper human communication, but even in the text, I could read the subtext. They were afraid for me—probably more afraid than they had been at any point since I went away to Virginia Tech for the first time.

"Are there storm shelters?" my mom typed.

"Not really," I said, hating to have to say it. "They gave us a class to prepare us, but we're kind of on our own. They advised going to the highest point possible, because the high points have less wind and water."

"And where will you go?"

"My friend Timi has a house way up on the hill. I'll be safe up there."

The truth was that I wasn't sure whether I'd be safe anywhere on the island, but I didn't want my mother going twenty-four hours without sleep while she fretted over the flimsiness of my plan. It was the only plan available to me, but still—if you grow up in a corner of the world where basements are common, as is the knowledge that the best place to take shelter from a storm is in your basement, it's hard to hear that your daughter plans to wait out what promises to be a giant and destructive hurricane on the highest point she can find on a mountain.

So I pivoted. "Jen and I are going to the store for canned goods as soon as she finishes getting ready," I wrote.

There was a long pause. "That's good," she said finally. "Make sure you get as much as possible. You don't know how long the aftermath will last."

My mom was right, I knew, but at the time, I didn't realize just how right. Her sentiment seemed to be the consensus on the island, because everywhere Jen and I went in search of canned food, we found the place had been picked clean already. The shelves at our local grocery were always pretty sparsely outfitted, but all we found on that day before the storm was dust and despair.

"Well, let's hope we don't starve after this thing hits," Jen said.

"Maybe it won't be as bad as they say."

Few Americans ever really have to experience the feeling so common in much of the rest of the world, but making a trip for food and not finding food is cripplingly depressing. That's especially true when you know that circumstances might prevent you from being able to get food for the next few days or even weeks. Our hurricane preparedness class had prepared us for the coming onslaught of wind and rain and flooding, but we found ourselves unprepared for the desperate grittiness of the aftermath.

In an effort to assuage that desperation, we picked through the supplies Michael had set up for us in the house prior to the day we moved in. There were batteries and flashlights and lanterns mostly.

"It's too bad you can't eat these things," I said to Jen as I fed a squat D battery into one of the flashlights.

We both had a scared little chuckle.

All around us, people were packing their outdoor items into their houses and hiding out behind closed storm shutters. If we couldn't make it up the mountain, all I would have was a bathtub to hide out in. Jen had one too, so we wouldn't have to share, at least. I still sometimes wonder how we would have made a one-tub scenario work, considering we also would have had to share the space with two big dogs and a kitten named after a volcano.

In the hours before the storm was to hit, the clouds were so dark that it became difficult to remember whether it was day or night. My family back home was as nervous as I can ever remember them being. Mom was a particular wreck. The internet was down, so the AOL option gave way to spending a small fortune on calling back home to give an update.

"Where are you?" Mom asked immediately.

"Still at home," I said.

"I thought you were going up the mountain to your friend's house."

"Timi's," I said too quickly. "Yes, I'm going to Timi's." The truth was that the storm already had me so afraid that I didn't know whether we'd make it. Timi lived in a part of the island called Mattingley Heights. In the back of a huge residence, her tiny apartment was essentially a storm shelter. I'd have had nothing to worry about at Timi's. Not during the storm anyway. It resided right next to the volcano, which was pretty high up. Really, a quick ride up the street from where I lived could've taken us where we needed to go, but at that moment, even just a quick ride up the street seemed impossible. Everyone had been saying that the storm would hit suddenly, but we never could have anticipated just how suddenly. It went from sunny to drizzling to heavy rains and wind to absolute chaos in a matter of an hour.

"And what if you can't make it to Timi's?"

"I'm going to take shelter in the bathtub."

In the silence, I could sense Mom's doubt.

"Michael, my landlord, says we'll be okay in the tub."

"There's nowhere you can go?" she would say, her voice shaky like maybe she was crying. The sound made it difficult for me to avoid crying too, but I knew I had to keep strong or one of us would lose it.

"This is the safest place right now. You should see these bathtubs. They're like tanks. And we'll have the mattresses to—"

"Just try to get to Timi's," she interrupted. "And if you can't, then please don't get out of that tub. But call when you can. We want updates whenever it's possible."

"Okay."

"What are you doing right now?"

I shrugged, even though I knew she couldn't see it. Cooper was curled up with Lia at the foot of the sofa. Jen was off in her room, packing some of her things and moving them closer to the center of the house, away from the walls and windows. Both of us had beers nearby and were grateful for the relative calm they brought. Outside, darkness reigned and the rain poured relentlessly. The mango and avocado trees in the yard had taken on a leaning, wind-blown posture. We had seen our share of tropical storms in my two-plus years at Ross, and that's pretty much exactly how this storm looked. I tried not to think about how much worse it could get.

"We're just hanging out," I said truthfully. "Waiting for a break in the storm so we can get up to Timi's."

It's difficult to hang up with someone you love when that someone is afraid you might not be safe. It took several more calling-card-covered minutes to grant my mom enough assurance to convince her all would be well.

But then, even I wasn't sure that all would be well. Up to the point when it felt like the wind was shaking the house right down to the foundation, I had handled it all just like a proper islander. What would be would be. In the meantime, I'd just amble around, gathering my stuff and slowly sipping my beer. But now, as I started herding Cooper and Lia toward the bathroom, I was scared. There would be no making it to Timi's. At least not yet. For now, the tub would have to do.

The three pets in the house were really confused. Fortunately, I had the chill-est dog on the planet, because otherwise the bathtub arrangement would have been untenable. Lia was no big fan of getting pulled into a big ceramic bowl and covered with an old mattress, but Cooper—who always wanted to be near me anyway—was as content as can be. We were two little bugs snug in a rug, and then also we had this tiny cat who wasn't at all snug and didn't mind showing it with her teeth and claws.

So that's how we spent the next couple of hours, packed like warm, furry sardines in a tin that smelled like it had absorbed about a decade of the distinct mothballs-and-old-perfume odor of Michael's house. That self-made fortress was crazy dark, and also terrifyingly quiet. When you're tucked in and waiting for a massive storm to hit, there's something strangely calming about being able to hear the wind and rain. I guess it's the notion that, as long as you can still hear that sound, and it sounds like it's still just happening outside the house instead of inside, you know for sure you're safe for the time being. But if you're holed up in a sound chamber covered with a mattress, all you hear is your dog's panting and your cat's mewling, bitey complaints.

It was a long afternoon.

Afterward, though, everything was fine—or at least as fine as an island can be after getting pummeled by tropical-storm-level winds and rain. Once it was safe to go outside again, Michael came by to check on us. Power and television had miraculously restored almost immediately, and our landlord had been watching the news.

"It hit Grenada," he said. "Turned at the last possible minute, or it would have hit us much harder."

"And Grenada?"

Michael just shook his head mournfully.

It would be a while before the true scope of the devastation surfaced, but the news could not have been grimmer. Hurricane Ivan's terrible surge and 125-mile-per-hour winds would destroy over thirty percent of the houses on that island, leaving 18,000 people homeless and killing thirty-nine. The damage was so significant that the island is still in many ways recovering to this day. Venezuela, Trinidad, and Barbados suffered casualties as well. Somehow, St. Kitts, which had stood so directly in the monster's path, had avoided it all.

Later, as soon as I could get a working phone line, I was thrilled to call my parents and put their worries to rest.

"You have no idea how relieved I am to hear your voice," my mom said, and I could hear that she was crying.

"Thanks, Mom," I said. "Turns out it was really just heavy rains and winds. There have been tropical storms that have caused more damage here."

"Did you hear about Granada?" my dad said, apparently having grabbed the other line upstairs.

"Hi, Dad. Yes, I heard. It's so terrible."

"We just kept thinking that if that had been you . . ." My mom trailed off into silence, and for the first time since the storm, I got a little choked up.

"I know," I said.

Cooper, as alert as he always was to my emotional state, lifted his head and gave me the side-eye as if trying to sort out whether he should come and provide comfort. He must have decided on yes, because soon after, he trotted over to plop his slobbery muzzle in my lap. I ran a hand over his head and to the back of his neck as I got back to soothing my parents' concerns.

"I, for one, am glad that this is your last hurricane season," Dad said.

"Oh, thank God," my mom said with such relief that it sounded like it was the only thing that allowed her any sleep at night.

I gave a teary-eyed laugh. "Less than two months. They don't have any hurricanes in West Lafayette, do they?"

My dad chuckled. "Maybe a tornado or two."

Not long before that moment, Lafayette, the town neighboring West Lafayette, where Purdue and my upcoming clinical year awaited, had been hit by a severe tornado. The thought made me break into goosebumps.

"Going to be different, that's for sure," Dad added. "And anyway, you'll be more likely to encounter an ice storm than a thunderstorm for the next three or four months, at least."

"Ugh," I groaned. "That sounds pleasant."

Yes, upon my return to the States, right after the Christmas break, I was set to take up residence in a locale with decidedly different weather patterns. Except for the weather, I was excited about Purdue. It would be hard work, I knew, but I had been working hard for long enough that I almost didn't remember what a genuinely lazy day looked like. This would be different, though. Every veterinary student has to complete a year of clinical rotations in different specialties at a hospital or clinic in an effort to expose him/her to the varied rigors of being a practicing veterinarian. They're usually extremely demanding, both in terms of the knowledge you're expected to absorb and the hours you're expected to work. Similarly to residencies for doctors, it's a bit like intellectual/emotional/professional boot camp. Unlike with residencies for doctors, you don't get paid. Purdue was a random assignment for me—you don't get to pick where you complete your clinical year—but it was (and is) a great school, so the part of me that wasn't nervous about the long year to come was really excited about the prospect of learning under some of the top minds in the field.

My excitement and anxiety were such that the final month-plus of my time in St. Kitts flew by in what felt like a week. Hurricane season was less eventful for our little pocket of the Caribbean, and the workload at school slackened enough that I had a chance to enjoy the eerily great weather that trailed the hurricane. I remember those days as exciting and nerve-racking and sad all mixed into one sourball of emotion. The ball expanded to its largest size two days before my graduating class was set to depart.

On that day, the university threw a goodbye party for the seniors. I'd been on the island for enough of these that I thought I had a vague idea of what to expect, but nothing could have prepared me for the sheer amount of laughter, good times, and tears. They held the thing at one of the luxury hotels on the island and stuffed our bellies to capacity in the banquet hall.

Awesome party. We all had a great time. But then, the reality really started to set in. Next came a blur of packing and taking my last looks at all my favorite spots. Then it was airport time.

When first I had come to the island—and for most of the two years that followed—American was the only airline that flew into St. Kitts, and it seemed like connection after connection to get me home. My friends dealt with the same issues getting back to their respective corners of the country. But in the lead-up to our final departure, we learned that US Airways had joined the fray, adding a direct flight from St. Kitts to Charlotte, North Carolina. For any of us from the Midwest or East, this was tremendous news, as it meant we could cut out at least one connecting flight. And since there was only one flight out on the day we were to depart, it also meant that all of us were on the same flight.

This made the goodbyes rather strange. The tears started almost immediately. And we all kept them on kind of a slow drip from St. Kitts to Charlotte. When you're in a moment like that, you tell yourself that it'll be easier to say goodbye to these great friends because we still have a few hours together on the plane. But in many ways, it's far easier to say goodbye once and be done with it. Any hours spent in transit with a person you know you won't see again for a long, long while are like hours from another dimension. It's as if that time doesn't really exist.

The whole thing was made weirder—mostly for the airline, I'm sure—because we were all soon-to-be veterinarians, which meant we all had at least one pet. Everyone getting on that plane had a dog or a cat in tow, and in many cases, both. I fell into that latter group, obviously, with my big new crate for Cooper and tiny new crate for Lia. In this way, we boarded a plane with what must have been the loudest, pet-smelliest cargo hold in the history of commercial flight. And then we spent the next handful of hours trying to cram in as much meaning as possible into our final conversations.

My friends would all be going to different corners of the country to complete their own clinical years. Plus, during that year, and even in the few years immediately after, we all expected to be working pretty much constantly. So there was a foreboding sense that it would be a long time before we would see each other again. In fact, it seemed almost likely that I would *never again* see some of my best friends on the island. We had grown to become something of a family, the lot of us. And now we would be breaking apart to pursue new lives, and eventually, new families of our own.

CHAPTER NINE

The Freeze

The transition from island to the States, and from a young woman with a family of vetschool friends to a young woman entering all nervously into her clinical year was stark. It didn't help that there are few transitions one can make on planet Earth that feature quite such a contrast in weather.

After all those weeks and months in tropical St. Kitts, I'll never forget what the flight attendant said over the intercom on my connecting flight from Charlotte to Pittsburgh just before we began our descent. He informed the date and time of our landing, the duration of our flight, and then drew a deep breath to prepare us for the temperature. My parents had told me to expect a cold snap, but there are cold snaps and there is the dark side of the moon. When the flight attendant informed us that, with the wind chill factored in, it felt like eighteen degrees below zero on the ground, a collective groan rippled through the cabin.

The daytime temperature when I departed that morning was eighty-five degrees. Clumsily I did the math. Touchdown would bring a swing of *99 degrees*.

My heart leapt when I came off the tram at Pittsburgh International Airport and saw my parents waiting for me at the head of the receiving line. They were giddy. They were huggy. They were warm and happy, and for me, they were home.

"Oh my God, you're so tan," my mom said.

It was true. Those last couple of weeks on the island had been relaxed enough study-wise that I'd been able to lie out quite a bit. My skin took on a deeper dark than I'd ever achieved, or ever would again. One guy on the island, in the process of hitting on me, I guess, told me that, with my blond hair and darker skin, I looked just like Mariah Carey. No one has ever mistaken me for her since that day.

"And you have Cooper!" my dad said.

I laughed. "Yeah, we got him off the plane this time. Which is nice."

We hugged again and gathered up all my stuff for the final leg of my journey home.

You hear about dramatic below-zero temperatures. A part of you even thinks maybe you've experienced them. But even if my blood hadn't been warmed for so long by island living, I'm confident that nothing could have prepared me for the reality of an eighteen-below wind chill. Stepping out through the sliding glass doors that separated baggage claim from the hellscape that Pittsburgh International had become, my eyes were instantly flash-frozen. The contents of my nose crystalized. My lips chapped the second they touched the impossible chill. My bones creaked and ached as if I'd aged ten years in an instant. From her cage, Lia sounded furious. Cooper, though, didn't even react. Dude was chill enough already, I guess, that a little cold wasn't going to bother him.

The snow was piled so high that I couldn't see the parking lot on the opposite side of the arrivals lanes. It seemed like it took half a day to get home, partly because Pittsburgh International is almost closer to the Ohio border than it is to actual Pittsburgh, and partly because it felt like even the car couldn't bear the cold. It was as if the tires had to unstick themselves from the frozen pavement with every inch. And even with the unearthly temperature, the snow just kept coming.

Back home finally, we moved me back in to my temporary living quarters in my parents' basement. For a while I was too keyed up to pay any attention to how my body was begging for sleep. It was so great to be home, to be safe, and to know that I would have another month to spend with family and old friends. Then there was the notion that this would likely be the last month-long Christmas break I would ever have. The thought filled me with a bittersweet sense that I had to cherish every moment.

Cooper was hilarious that evening. He kept wandering the house as if searching for something he had misplaced. Every few minutes or so, he would plop down in some corner of the room or at my feet and just pant happily. I might've worried that this was the lead-up to a seizure, but it had been so long since his last one that the truth was, I didn't worry about them quite as constantly. His drugs had leveled him out so well that mostly I just worried about making sure I kept to the complex routine of rolling his food and pills down his throat. As long as I did that, there were no problems to report.

At some point it occurred to me that Cooper was particularly peppy that night because this wasn't the same kind of homecoming for him—not the same as it was for me, anyway. He was born in North Carolina, had lived with me briefly at Virginia Tech, had enjoyed stops in Pittsburgh at several intervals, and had spent the bulk of his young life living on a sunny island. I wasn't sure whether it was due to his perpetually cool disposition or to all this moving around, but Cooper seemed happy and at home just about anywhere. More likely, the truth was that he was so into me that it didn't matter where we set up our beds. As long as we were together, he didn't care what part of the planet we occupied. He just loved his mom. And his mom was home.

That thought eliminated my worry that he would have any trouble adjusting to life at Purdue. Besides, I figured if the guy could make it several hours in a bathtub covered by a mattress, Indiana would be no problem. Of course I still felt bad for having to move him again, but he always seemed to know just how to ease any guilt I might've carried. One slobbery smile, and all my troubles melted away.

So we passed that first evening and into the night catching up with my parents and avoiding the unforgiving elements raging in the outside world. Eventually, though, my parents had to go to bed, and Cooper couldn't wait any longer to brave the cold and relieve himself. So I said my goodnights to Mom and Dad, threw on a thick coat, and stepped out to hook Cooper to the chain that would keep him in the yard. I figured he wouldn't want to be out there for more than two seconds, but he darted away into the darkness just like he always did—as if nothing in the world was the matter with minus-eighteen degrees wind chill.

He did return a little sooner than usual, but that smile of his never broke.

I don't know how it happened. One moment, I was climbing into bed after setting Cooper up in his crate, and the next Cooper was barking me awake. Somehow, night had progressed to dawn in the time it took me to blink. I was still so exhausted from the long journey that I almost fell asleep again before I could let Cooper out. He wasn't having that, though, so I reluctantly rose, released him from his crate, and stepped for the door.

Whether it was grogginess or just force of habit created by living on a tropical island for over two years I can't say, but I didn't think to put on a coat, or even a pair of socks before sliding on my shoes.

The cold nearly knocked me down.

"C'mon, Cooper," I tried to say, but my teeth were chattering too hard to get it out as anything more than a rapid firing of hard consonant sounds.

Together we shuffled out to the tree, where I found the impossibly cold chain crusted up in ice. I kicked it free and somehow managed to secure the latch over the buckle on Cooper's collar. Then I shuffled back to the door.

I was shaking all over by the time I got back to the warmth of the basement. There was nothing I could do but crawl back into bed and cover up. Lying on my side, I shivered for a while, cursing myself for my stupidity. Then a warm wave came over me—the blanket and the blessed HVAC doing their jobs—and the shivering stopped.

That's the last thing I remember.

When I woke, I was immediately aware of how much lighter it was out the basement window above my bed. I experienced the briefest moment of dreamy confusion before I realized what had happened. I shot out of bed, fully alert and completely devastated.

Oh my God, Cooper, was my first thought. It was impossibly cold outside. I checked the clock by the door. Cooper had spent three hours in minus-eighteen degrees. I didn't want to admit it to myself, but surely my dear Cooper was dead. Every muscle tensed as I reached for my coat and made my way to the door.

Between the fear, the guilt, and the screamingly cold wind, my voice was shaky when I called out to him. "Cooper, I'm so sorry!"

When my friend didn't come bounding back, I sensed the worst. I imagined finding him under some snowdrift, his fur thick and stiff with frost, his eyes like blue crystal and unblinking. I'm not sure if I cried as I searched for him, because any tears I'd have produced would've frozen to my face.

All the snow meant a long search. It took me a while to reach the tree and then to find enough of the chain to riddle out its direction. Parts of the chain were frozen directly to the frosted grass under the snow, so I had to tug my way ever closer to the end to which I had tied Cooper. I grew shorter of breath with every tug, fearing that any moment I would stumble across a popsicle that had once been my puppy. But then I reached the end and found something I hadn't expected. The latch where I had secured Cooper's collar was held open by frost. Cooper was nowhere to be found.

As quickly as one's mind can work in that kind of cold, I reasoned that the latch must have frozen and broken off. There was no telling how long ago this had happened, but it least explained why Cooper hadn't returned to the door to holler me awake. He always was a wanderer.

I felt a surge of dread and, simultaneously, hope. On one side, my dog had wandered off, and there was no way to know which direction he had gone because the wind had blown enough snow to cover whatever tracks he may have made. On the other, I had not in fact found a puppy popsicle in the yard. That meant there was a chance—however slim—that he had found a way to survive the Antarctic-grade cold.

So I returned to the house, bundled up further, and went out in search of my friend.

I didn't get far before recognizing how insane it was to perform this search on foot. There is cold and there is *cold*. This was something else entirely. So I rushed back to the house and feverishly started calling around to places he might have wound up. Animal shelters. Police stations. Vet clinics. Anywhere that a good Samaritan might take a shivering, lost dog. No one had seen him. Then I remembered his collar. He was tagged with my cellphone number, so at least whoever found him would be able to call me. Even so, I rushed to put together a flyer that I could print out and post all over the neighborhood. The flyers featured a close-up picture of Cooper sitting, his big eyes adorable. Across the top, I'd printed "LOST" in enormous, bold caps.

By 10am, I was out in my Jeep, the heat blasting as I drove block by block in search of signs of my friend. At each new block, I would get out, walk for a bit, and yell as loudly as I could. I would post my flyers on any sensible surface I could find.

The search proved fruitless. Eight, ten, and then twelve hours had passed. I was inconsolable. With everything Cooper had endured, and all the lengths the two of us had gone to in an effort to give him a happy life, one incredibly dumb mistake was what had ended it all. I had tried so hard to help him beat the odds, and in the end, I'd fallen asleep and let him freeze to death. The thought was more than I could stand.

Then, after twelve hours of beating myself up, my mom came skipping down to my bedroom, phone in hand. From the glow of her, my heart warmed with hope.

"Hello?"

"Hey, is this Katti?"

I began twisting my hair over my finger. "Yes."

"I saw your flyer," the impossibly comforting voice said. "I think I have your dog in my living room."

An awesome wave of relief crashed over me. I rushed to grab a pen and paper, then furiously began jotting down the details of where and when I could find my missing friend. As it turned out, Cooper's hound-dog tendency to follow his nose without paying attention to where he was going had sent him a full five miles away from our house. The family that found him had encountered him in their back yard, playing with their puppy.

"It's a good thing for that flyer," the woman told me. "Because when we found him and saw his collar, we just couldn't believe he was from around here."

"Oh? Why's that?"

"Well, it's just that 'WI' he had on his tags, you see. We thought he'd somehow run here all the way from Wisconsin."

I laughed along with her but figured it would be better not to tell her that the truth was slightly more mundane— that he had only run five miles, and that "WI," in this case, stood for "West Indies."

I hopped into the Jeep and took off in the direction of the address the woman had given me. It was a long five miles through the rolling hills so common in the Pittsburgh area. The farther I went, the more I marveled at how in the world Cooper could've followed a scent this far, let alone through this kind of winding, forested terrain.

The house he'd wandered into presented as a modest, redbrick place with a nice porch on the front. I knocked, and found a pleasant family awaiting me. The mother and father were quite happy and relieved to see me, but it was clear that the three young kids weren't as thrilled, as they seemed to have fallen in love with Cooper already.

"He was just so cute that we couldn't let him stay out there," the mother told me. "I could see he had a collar but didn't have a chance to call the number because we were literally on our way out the door to a Christmas concert."

"We just figured we'd leave him at home for now and call the number later," the father said.

"It's okay." I smiled as Cooper nuzzled up to me as if nothing had happened. "I'm just glad he found a good family to keep him safe."

"Pretty cold out there," the father said. "I can't believe he made it all this way."

I agreed. Cooper bounded off to play with the children and their puppy. That left me with the parents to discuss our general shock that such a journey was even possible, never mind the cold. The father showed me how, in the back of the house, there was a sliding glass door that led into the kitchen. If not for that door, the family might not have seen Cooper playing with their puppy before he decided to follow that scent elsewhere.

"It's just a Christmas miracle, I guess," the mother said.

With that thought bringing a smile to my face, I watched my dog bound after a ball that one of the children had thrown. The kids all laughed uproariously as he batted and flailed at it with his clumsy paws. *My own little Christmas miracle*, I thought.

• • •

We'd tried to sell the old red Jeep Cherokee that month while I was home, but for some reason, couldn't find any takers. So there we were, packing it to the brim yet again with all the stuff I would need for another move to another university. Parting with my family this time was easier. When you live overseas for any significant period, traveling just a couple states away doesn't stir quite the same homesickness it might have before.

So it was with a "see you later" sort of casualness that I parted from my family and drove my pets and worldly belongings to West Lafayette, Indiana. It was slow going, because my curse with disastrous weather had not yet expired, apparently. The chill and snow of Pennsylvania broke somewhere in the middle of Ohio and became sheets of shockingly slick ice. I kept the pedal at an angle that had the engine on crawl.

Eventually, after what felt like a couple of days, we got there, and all in one piece.

The place where I would take up residence during the clinic rotation was a single-floor townhouse in a complex called Cheswick Village. The spaces were modern and new and occupied mostly by graduate students. It was a safe, quiet, well-manicured neighborhood—certainly a stark contrast to the one I had been living in during vet school.

And at least the snow was gone. Unfortunately, that ice storm had tagged along all the way to our new home, so my pet-family and I had to choose our steps carefully. Trouble was that Cooper had never done anything terribly careful in his whole life. There are many memories I will recall from my time at Purdue, but I think the most indelible will always be from that first night. I let Cooper out to do his business, and the ice was so thick that it had transformed the grassy yard into a solid sheet of ice. If you've ever seen a five-year-old trying to ice skate for the first time, you have a pretty good idea of what Cooper looked like while trying to engage in his potty time. It was all he could do to keep those big old paws of his from sliding in four different directions. He must have face planted three times before he finally got the hang of it. And even then, he would flop his paws clumsily, one in front of the other, and skid a foot or two farther than he had intended. Even when he got down into his BM-crouch, his momentum kept carrying him to where he was pooping in motion. I could've sold tickets. "English Foxhounds on Ice." Even Lia seemed to think it was funny.

Eventually I took pity on him and put on my shoes to help, but I wasn't much better out there. The ice was unbelievable. It was the smoothest, shiniest, slickest rink you can imagine. No Zamboni could ever hope to create such slippery glass. And it coated everything. Light posts, road signs, the fence around our yard, every car—right down to the antenna. It was as if the world had become a collection of giant icicles. When I reached down to try to get my uncoordinated dog back on his feet, I fell too. The two of us slid around together for a minute or two before I crawled and pawed my way back inside to help with encouragement instead.

It took another couple of minutes, but Cooper finally did get back into the house. And the moment he stepped inside, he just trotted off with that champion strut of his, as if thinking, *Yeah, nobody saw that, right? I can still do this.*

After the weather cleared up to where I could get out of the house again, I quickly learned that the best part about our new home was that the drive to campus took five minutes. I would spend pretty much all of my waking hours there over the year to come. I probably could have used a job for the extra money, but there was absolutely no time. My first rotation was at the hospital, where we handled emergencies, large-animal medicine, and surgery. Some days, I'd be in there twenty-three out of twenty-four hours. There were times when I went forty-eight hours without sleeping. Then, after one of those stretches, I'd be let loose to go home and crash for a while. Even then, I wouldn't be off the hook, as I'd get called back in whenever an emergency case showed up in the middle of the night. These middle-of-the-night emergencies usually involved horses, so the emergency of the situation was clear. I'd go from enjoying my second hour of sleep to being scrubbed in for an eight-hour surgery in about fifteen total minutes of prep and drive time.

This is all to say that my first clinic rotation was a proper hell. Even the average day was sixteen hours, but the biggest adjustment was all the time on my feet. The clinic itself was so large that the other residents and I would wear pedometers just to see how far we walked each day. The average was eight miles. So here I would be at the end of walking fourteen to sixteen miles at the end of a forty-four-hour shift, and I'm supposed to keep myself awake while I finish up some paperwork about the past two days of cases.

The other two rotations—pathology and small-animal medicine—were quite a bit easier, but they weren't picnics either. Small animal, for instance, would have me on my feet for fifteen hours, then a two-hour break at home before getting called back in. On this rotation, there was also the distraction of having to manage the care of ICU patients.

Plus, there was the studying. Aspiring vets on their clinic rotations still have to take exams. This meant that, if I wasn't at the clinic, I was mostly just studying. If I wasn't studying, I was preparing my cases for the next day or figuring out what was going on with a horse whose maladies we had yet to explain. Then, running on an improbably small amount of sleep, I'd stand there in clinics before a firing squad of professors who would drill me and the other residents on the details we were expected to know. There were dozens of patients—sometimes it felt like hundreds—and the expectation was that I would know everything going on with all of them.

And this is all just to become a general practitioner of veterinary medicine. If a student wants to further specialize, he or she completes another year on an internship and then chooses a residency in his/her specialty to undertake for another three years. For this reason, I, like many vet students, elected not to specialize.

To me, though, my own suffering during this period of my life mattered far less than what I perceived to be Cooper's suffering. He was always happy to see me in those short stretches when I was home—and of course I always made sure to keep him covered with visits and opportunities to go outside with volunteers who would come and let him out—but that new environment with all the infrequent attention it entailed kind of led Cooper to act out. And by "kind of," I mean that Cooper's behavior trended toward disastrous.

His separation anxiety at first caused him to start peeing on the floor just about every day. I ended up having to put tarps down on the floor. Every day, I would get home and find puddles of urine scattered all around the blue plastic tarps. Every night, I would have to take them outside and hose them off before setting them back out again. I often caught my neighbors looking out their back windows to get a load of what I was doing. They must have thought I was crazy. That didn't bother me, though. What bothered me was that I couldn't come up with a better solution to fight the problem at its source. Separation anxiety is a difficult thing for a dog to manage. His emotional state had to have been in constant flux. He was so attached to me that, whenever I got home, he would be *beyond* excited. I would try to take him out to play whenever I could—and we bonded hard during those short periods—but those occasions were too few and too far between. He became close to my friend Dawn, the most frequent of the volunteers who would come and take him out during the day. And he had Lia to keep him at least somewhat occupied. But, man, his life had gone from sunshine and mango tree shade to crazy-cold temperatures outside and confinement to the house for twenty-three-or-so hours a day.

So the unwanted peeing didn't really slow down no matter what I tried. And as the days and weeks slogged by, Cooper started taking out his frustrations on the house itself. His anxiety eventually assumed the form of

impulsive hunger. Of course it didn't help that his medications gave him the munchies. He would get into the
garbage, the drawers, the cabinets, *everything*. Eventually
I had the place so locked up and baby-proofed, I could've
opened a daycare—provided, of course, that my clientele
didn't mind all the dog pee.

But even these drastic measures proved insufficient.
One day, I came home to find that everything that had
been in the refrigerator was no longer in the refrigerator.
And I do mean everything. It was like the Mother's Day
brunch all over again. He had eaten a pound of frozen
chicken. He had wolfed down an entire carton of ice
cream. A pound of ground beef. What was left of a carton
of eggs. The ketchup and mustard had been chewed open
and feasted upon. Etc. It was the *entire fridge*.

My initial reaction was entirely visceral. It was disbelief. Horror. Something akin to, "Oh my God! I can't
believe this happened." Then followed the terror. When
you see a dog literally wallowing in pounds of people food,
pretty much right away you start to worry about toxicity.

Pancreatitis was the word that jumped into my head.
My brain was still too overwhelmed to piece together
everything about what that meant, but I did know that
the situation could be life threatening. Absently I rushed
for the door, grabbing my car keys and kind of half-throw-
ing my coat over my shoulders before remembering that
I should probably gather my dog to leave. My fear and
frustration and love and anger were so powerful all at once
that my body had started working on the plan before my
conscious mind had even put it together.

When finally my conscious mind caught up to me, my first cogent thought was that my body had been right: I had to drive Cooper to the clinic as quickly as possible. My second thought was that the clinic was just about the last place in the world I wanted to be after a forty-hour shift. My third thought was that no matter what they told me about how to deal with the situation, Cooper was about to have a day or two of the most interesting bowel movements he'd ever had.

If I were going to give the vets all the information they would need, though, I had to assess the damage. What, exactly, had Cooper eaten, and in roughly what quantities? So I started taking an inventory. The truly puzzling thing was how he had managed to get into the freezer, which was top loading. I mean, when he stood on his hind legs, he matched all five feet and two inches of me, but even I had trouble reaching the back of that freezer. Somehow, he had gotten onto his hind legs and positioned himself with enough support to nose the freezer door open, then wormed his way into the depths to gather every last morsel of its contents. I wish I'd had a camera. I would love to have seen that on film.

If I hadn't been so concerned by the notion that my dog had just eaten his way into pancreatitis, I might have been a little amazed. As I rushed him to the clinic, it occurred to me that Cooper was probably going to be fine—by that point, I had treated enough dogs that had played garbage disposal for an evening to know exactly what I would learn once we arrived at the clinic.

"I don't know if I'm going to survive these rotations,"

I said sarcastically to Cooper as he rested in the backseat of my Jeep, contentedly licking crusted ketchup off his paws, "but I do know that I'm learning a whole lot from being your mother."

Thankfully, Cooper had a stomach of steel, or my nightly tarp-washing routine would have looked even more disturbing for the week that followed. But in the end, he was right as rain—as if nothing had ever happened. I did have to put child locks on my refrigerator and freezer. When a few days later, he proved that he had figured out how to open them, I added a second lock to each door. He solved that setup too. So I added a third. That proved to be the trick, not because he couldn't reason it out, but because by the time he got the first two sets of locks open, he'd be too tired to work on the third.

So that's how my house started to look like it belonged to a paranoid schizophrenic who feared the government could read her thoughts through her pantry doors. Every door had at least one lock. In terms of its complication, the process for opening the refrigerator called to mind the process for launching a nuclear warhead. Everywhere I turned, there was an obstacle to move or climb over. Every door had a gate. Every gate had a lock. Every lock sometimes had a companion lock.

And even that couldn't contain him.

Lia, like most cats, did all her pooping in the comfort of my climate-controlled apartment. We kept a litter box for her in the laundry area. By the time of the incident, still not long after the move, I had already started building my sophisticated network of barriers to keep Cooper out of trouble. Or so I thought. The litter box was up high enough—and seemed unappetizing enough—that I figured Cooper wouldn't ever mess with it. I was wrong. Sure enough, he was able to climb to where he could get to it.

Big deal, right? Dogs eat poop all the time. Cooper used to eat it straight from his own source of the stuff. But it wasn't the cat feces that was the problem. It was the clumping cat litter. Part of how this particular brand of litter keeps the cat-pee-smell at a minimum is that it's designed to clump and create a solid mass when mixed with liquid. So now instead of cat pee, you've got a pleasantly scented rock of cat pee. But what happens when you eat it? There are all sorts of liquids in your stomach that wouldn't do so well if clumped into a rock. When a dog swallows a significant amount of kitty litter, it can clump into huge *piles* of rocks that he can't pass on his own and he winds up needing surgery to remove it.

One look at the scene when I got home that day said that, yes, my dog had swallowed a significant amount of kitty litter. Immediately I got down to doing what I do best in situations involving my own pets: freaking out. As a fourth-year student, I was learning every day how completely calm I always was when dealing with a crisis involving someone else's animal. But I guess I've always had more trouble removing the emotional when it comes to my own animals. And Cooper especially.

My first instinct was to call the emergency hospital, but then I remembered the bills. It had been a few weeks since our last trip to the ER, but I could still see the number I arrived at in my calculator after totaling up all my credit card balances just after that event. It was in the neighborhood of $7,000. With the benefit of hindsight, that doesn't seem such an astronomical sum, but for a veterinary resident with no time for a job and almost no money in the bank, it might as well have been $7 *million*.

So when that number flashed in my head, I hung up and decided to try the quicker, cheaper option first. I had made friends with a girl who had been a resident in the program at Purdue for nearly a year at that point, and she just so happened to be specializing in the very problem for which I figured Cooper might be facing.

"Give it forty-eight hours," she suggested.

"Forty-eight hours?"

"I know it seems terrifying, but you have to give him time to tell you whether there's actually anything wrong. He might just pass it."

The "it," in this case, meant the stomach-acid-stones the kitty litter was likely filling him with. I thanked my friend, hung up, and returned to staring at Cooper for any sign of discomfort. I'd like to say that it was because I didn't have the time to keep him under personal observation for forty-eight hours, but the truth was that I couldn't stand to wait any longer than forty-eight *minutes*. So I rushed him to the ER at the university and pulled as many strings as I could to get him an X-ray ASAP.

I remember watching Cooper lick his paws, oblivious, as we awaited the results. If he hadn't looked so serene and adorable, I might've been mad at him. But how can someone be mad at someone they love so unconditionally? Only a pet owner can understand this, I think, because even with parenting, it's possible to hold on to that anger for an hour or two. But with a pet you love, given that he/she can't help him/herself, it's impossible to be angry for more than a couple of minutes. Really, it only lasts for however long it takes to clean up the mess.

When the door swung open, it turned out the person holding the X-rays was the same friend I had called for advice.

"Should've waited forty-eight hours." She showed me the films.

We lucked out on that one. Cooper had clearly eaten some litter, but he hadn't managed to block anything. It would just be a matter of waiting out some more strange poops.

• • •

One day while on rotation, I happened to pass one of those cork boards you see all over college campuses, so decked out with flyers that it's like a three-dimensional mass of paper. One flyer caught my eye, announcing an upcoming lecture by a visiting veterinarian who specialized in neurology. It advertised him as one of the leading authorities on the subject. My surprise on reading the name was substantial. This was the same neurologist who had diagnosed Cooper with Lysosomal Storage Disease back at Virginia Tech.

I noted the time of the lecture, but then also realized that the flyer mentioned how the neurologist would be visiting the campus and contributing to some rotations with the small-animal medicine clinic over the weekend. So the first chance I got, I sought him out.

I could see a sense of vague recollection on his face.

"Do you remember me? I guess it's been over three years or so now."

He drew a breath and paused as if trying to gather a hint.

"I brought a purebred English Foxhound in to see you. His name's Cooper. You diagnosed him with Lysosomal Storage Disease."

"Absolutely!" he said, now looking like he remembered completely. "I was so sorry to have to give that diagnosis."

"Well, he's doing well."

His eyes went wide. "Are you kidding me? Cooper is still alive?"

I couldn't hide my pride. "He's over three years old now."

"I wouldn't have expected him to survive past a year!"

My smile broadened as I nodded. "I remember."

He went on to ask me about all the medications I had been giving him and everything I had done to keep him alive for so much longer than the expectation.

"That's truly amazing, Katti," he said. "Not everyone would be willing to take such care of their dog. And you've given him a high quality of life in the process. I'm very impressed."

That was probably one of my proudest moments as a vet student: thoroughly impressing one of the top minds in the field.

Then, one of the top minds in the field got serious. "Is it possible my original diagnosis was wrong?"

Now I felt like the vet student again. Reflexively I checked the charts I was holding, then realized that I wasn't getting grilled on rounds. The neurologist smiled.

"I'd like to run some more tests, if you think Cooper would be up for it."

I laughed. "I think Cooper would be thrilled just to get out of the house at this point."

"Oh, I know," he said, going on to share a few stories about how difficult it had been for him to keep a dog during his residency for the neurology specialty.

So the next day, I brought Cooper in for some blood tests. When those tests didn't show anything particularly definitive, the neurologist asked me a battery of questions about what kinds of tests had been run on Cooper in the past. He was pretty surprised to learn all the details about Cooper's checkered history at veterinary clinics and emergency rooms, and even more perplexed that no one had brought any new information that could help us figure out Cooper's situation.

"How many seizures was he having when I first diagnosed him?"

I shared the number. He wrote it down.

"And how many is he having now?"

I shared the number. He wrote it down.

In great detail, we discussed Cooper's case, regimen of drugs, and quality of life. The neurologist was fascinated and even a little amused by the incredibly meticulous notes I kept in my journal of Cooper's various conditions and run-ins with the ER.

In the end, he decided that Cooper's condition must

have been even rarer than the one he had diagnosed him with more than three years prior.

"It could be something called Cryptogenic Epilepsy," the neurologist said. "I just can't believe he's still alive. It's so amazing."

I didn't really have an explanation. I had done quite a lot to keep him going and had sacrificed much of my freedom as a twenty-something, not to mention the damage I had done to my credit score, but none of that mattered. I loved Cooper so completely that I would have done it ten times over and back again. But the truth was that none of that would have mattered if Cooper hadn't been Cooper.

"My dog isn't like just any dog," I said. "My dog is so happy, and so loving, that it doesn't matter what's going on with his bloodwork. He's still alive because he loves life so much."

I don't know if the answer only served to deepen the neurologist's confusion, or to inspire him. But I know how it made me feel to speak those words. Cooper and I had shattered expectations about his life expectancy. And as far as I was concerned, as long as his quality of life remained high, we would continue doing exactly that.

CHAPTER TEN

Aspirations

The winter of 2004/2005 brought with it a tumultuous time for Cooper. In December, my old buddy got to celebrate Christmas and nearly his birthday in the ICU back in Pittsburgh while I was home between my departure from St. Kitts and my start at Purdue. It was a story I had seen before, but the whole thing wasn't any less scary. Cooper managed to aspirate and wound up in the hospital with pneumonia.

I'll never forget the scene: Cooper lying in his cage in the ICU, tubes running into his nose, tail pounding the floor in his excitement to see me. I entered bearing gifts—an armful of wrapped presents and even a stocking I would hang on his cage. When I'd first walked in, he had looked a little lethargic, but the moment he saw me, he was his old self again. I got to spend an hour or two with him that day. I let him out of his cage and presented him with his gifts, which he bounced around excitedly.

His favorite present was the large bone wrapped with a bow. He chewed on that thing for most of the time I was with him.

"I tell you what, Cooper, for a dog with pneumonia, you sure have a lot of energy."

And that was Cooper, after all. Nothing the fates threw at him could break his stride. Seizures, pneumonia, various overconsumption incidents—none of it bothered him at all. He had spent many days in and out of hospitals, and he was still the happiest dog you were ever likely to meet.

"I just hope you're out of here by your birthday," I told him.

Good old Cooper managed to put my concerns to rest just in time. As it turned out, he received his discharge just a day or two before his fourth birthday. *Fourth* birthday. As the occasion approached, I couldn't help but marvel anew at how completely we had shattered the ceiling on his life expectation. If the neurologist from VT had been correct in his estimate, Cooper should have been dead for at least three years. This meant that the latest celebration of Cooper's birthday would be even bigger than the last, and bigger still than the one before that and the one before that. I stopped short of hiring a clown or renting a bounce-house, but there was no shortage of cake and gifts and party guests, and I still belted far louder than anyone else I subjected to singing the Happy Birthday song.

This celebration felt somewhat different, because although he had made it another year, in the back of my mind I was still concerned about the fragility of his life, given the seizing and the aspiration pneumonia. I always calmed at the sight of that happy smile of his, though, and the way he always managed to bounce back to 100% Cooper no longer than a day after any admission into the hospital. There were times when I questioned whether I should still be doing everything I was to keep Cooper alive, but then I'd watch him bound through the house, maul a birthday cake, or sidle up to a friend or family member for a good round of petting, and I would know: there was nothing I could or should have done differently. Cooper had no business being alive, but everything we had done had ensured that his quality of life was extraordinarily high.

These little affirmations would carry me just long enough to get us to Cooper's next incident. It was always something with that guy. The latest round happened just a month prior to my graduation from Purdue in January 2006. It was January 8th to be exact, when Cooper contributed to one of the longest days of my life. The rotation I was on with the internal medicine clinic was so demanding timewise that they gave me the green light to bring Cooper into the clinic during the day so he didn't have to be home and lonely/destructive all the time. He loved this new arrangement, as he got to chill in the kennel at the hospital, where they had a super fun dog run.

I was on a rotation when a friend in the program stopped me mid-stride.

"Hey, I was just in the kennel, and Cooper doesn't look so good."

I could feel myself turn white. "What do you mean?"

"He's just not really responsive."

I sought immediate permission for a break and went to check on him. And it was absolutely true. He was lethargic and his breathing was shallow, but the real kicker was when I offered him a treat and he didn't want it. Cooper had never refused food in his life, so I knew something was wrong. The sight caused flashbacks to his other bouts with pneumonia, so I quickly gathered him up and started him down the hall toward the ICU. Once I had him checked in, another friend who happened to be on a residency as a specialist took a listen to Cooper's lungs.

"Yeah," she said. "I hear crackling."

My heart sank, because I knew that meant he had pneumonia again.

A few X-rays and other tests later and, yes, he had aspiration pneumonia.

But how? I wondered. Cooper hadn't had access to any food while he was in the kennel. What in the world could he have aspirated?

Then an image flashed into my head: It was of Cooper, standing in my back yard, his mouth wide open and facing his rear end as he fed himself in a gross and entirely bizarre little loop I would later come to refer to as "snowconing." I had an image of my dog eating his own feces straight from the source, in other words.

It was strange behavior, to be certain. I always believed it was the drugs he was on that made him so hungry as to want to do this, but whatever the case, that was his one less-than-show-doggy habit. And what it meant was that Cooper, on that kennel-bound day in January, had eaten his own poop and aspirated it. Gross, obviously, but also terrifying, as poop contains a ton of bacteria—that is, after all, why it's poop—which was now hanging out in his lungs.

That was the terrible news. The bad news was that I was nearing the end of a really long shift, and my mind was running on empty already. The good news, though, was that we were already at the hospital—Purdue's teaching hospital, to be exact. So Cooper could not have found himself in a better place to aspirate his poop, or poop-spirate, as it were. The hospital had a sizable ICU with all the bells and whistles. It was a sterile environment, a long, rectangular room lined with stainless steel cages on one side and dog runs on the other. Every cage had IV fluid pumps and breathing apparatus. There was a pharmacy just outside the ICU. The place kept busy, too, with techs, residents, and some of the world's most knowledgeable doctors always flying around. Cooper found himself in a life-threatening situation, but at least it had occurred in the best possible place.

The difficult part was how different Cooper was during this stay than he had been in previous stays. Whenever someone would ask me why I kept fighting so hard to keep Cooper going after all he'd been through, I would always say that his quality of life remained remarkably high. From the outside looking in, I could see how it might seem as though I was just kind of dragging him along for my own selfish reasons—like maybe I just loved him too much to let him go, no matter how he might be suffering. But the truth was that, even with all those hospital visits, he didn't seem to suffer in the slightest. Even when he was drugged, or just out of surgery, or having to deal with a seizure or pneumonia or gastrointestinal discomfort, he behaved as if the world was just so very super fun. It made the decision easy. Every time. It wasn't me that kept Cooper going. It was Cooper's joy that kept him going.

This hospital stay, he was sicker than usual. He was often more lethargic than I was used to seeing. The stay stretched on for weeks. He had oxygen running into his snout via tubes, and there were IV pumps that had to be changed on the regular. Even so, he would sometimes perk up and be the old Cooper again, but the interim periods of exhaustion were longer than I would've liked to see.

Even though in the back of my mind I began to think that maybe it was time to let go—that maybe his lethargy made it official that I was pushing this too far—I did everything I could to keep him comfortable. I stuffed his cage full of blankets and pillows. I always made sure he had the foods and pills he needed and wanted. And since I remained the center of his universe, I spent as much time by his side as I could.

Then there was Clementine the basset hound. Paired with Cooper, I can't imagine two dogs on the planet more alike in terms of their veterinary history. They shared a birth year, general diagnosis, and general wellbeing at the time. Clementine seized in exactly the same way and with exactly the same frequency as Cooper. She also had a similar laundry list of run-ins with area vet clinics. Through Clementine, I met, for the first time in my life, people who could truly identify with the struggle. Clementine's owners had remortgaged their home twice to pay for their dear friend's increasingly expensive veterinary care. When you get to the point where you're in the ICU at Purdue, you know you're going to spend a ton of money. That's just a fact. And these two people were going to spend the money, no matter what.

So here, at least, we had two peas in a pod. We turned that ICU into about the most low-energy playdate one might imagine. This meant we would let Cooper and Clementine hang out together in one or the other's cage. Clementine's owners and I would commiserate often about the cost of this hospital stay, and more importantly, about how the love of a dog can impact one's head and one's heart. Independently, the three of us had started to think we were crazy for doing what we were doing, but at least now we could see that other crazy people like us existed.

This turned out to be a particularly severe bout of pneumonia. There was a long downward spiral where he got sicker than he had ever been. I came very close to convincing myself that the time had come to just let my best friend go. He had suffered enough, I reasoned, so there was no sense in making him suffer any more. But then I decided to try one last thing, because yes this was pneumonia, but it was fixable.

Along with his vets, we decided that if Cooper was going to pull through, then the final course of action would be to place a tube that would serve as a direct port into his stomach. The tube would go through the skin in his side, past his ribs, and into his belly. This would allow us to bypass his esophagus, which was causing the issue, and feed him and administer his meds by the most direct route possible.

"This has to be the last resort," I said. "I love him and want to keep him alive, but if he's not going to be happy or will be in pain, then it just wouldn't be right to continue."

His vets agreed.

"I can't stress this enough, though, Katti," the lead vet said, and since she happened to be one of the most knowledgeable doctors I had ever spoken to, I made sure to listen closely. "We're taking a huge risk by putting him under anesthesia."

I wished it could have been any other way, but I knew it was true. Cooper had pneumonia, and if your lungs aren't working properly, going under anesthesia is never advisable. But this was life or death, so there was nothing else we could do.

"The odds are still good that he won't make it."

"I know," I said, preparing myself for the worst.

At that point, I figured we had come so far, I couldn't imagine going out without trying to help him in any way possible. Yes, the procedure would cost gobs of money, but screw the money. I knew I had to spend whatever it took. I loved him more than anything. *Let's give Cooper his stomach tube and see what happens*, I thought. And that was how I found myself whipping out the overextended credit card one more time so that a team of some of the world's most amazing vets could make a last valiant effort to return Cooper to health and happiness.

All through the surgery, I paced the halls. I was a nervous wreck. I chewed my nails down to their nubs. The hour that passed felt like a week. But then the door to the OR swung open, and out strode the lead doc. She nodded that all had gone well.

"He responded well to the anesthesia. Better than I thought he would, actually. And we got the tube in. Now we just wait for him to wake and see how he's doing."

As soon as I received my clearance to go in and see him, I found a semi-conscious Cooper lying flat on his side, this strange plastic tube sticking out of his freshly shaved left lateral side. I had a hard time holding it together.

"Oh, Cooper." Normally I would've started by assuring him that I was there and giving him a kiss on the head, but on this occasion, I felt flattened by how helpless and weak and sick he looked. For the first time, I feared that this would be the last health saga I would help him endure.

Cooper did wake up that day, and after a few feedings and a couple rounds of meds, he did seem quite a bit better. But the lethargy remained, and that tube in his side was just so brutal to look at. It was the first real and constant visual reminder that my dog was ailing, and I had a hard time dealing with it. I knew he couldn't have been in better hands, but I still couldn't shake the thought that I had done something wrong or could be doing more. It made it difficult to concentrate on my rotation, which at the time was with the internal medicine department, one of the most demanding rotations in the program.

There is no denying that I was learning a lot, though. Cooper's latest battle proved to be only one of about a million ways that he was the best possible learning experience I ever could have asked for as an aspiring vet. When I wasn't on rotation, I was checking in on one of the direst and most exotic cases in the ICU, and that case happened to be a dog I loved dearly. Such was the intrigue behind Cooper's situation that he actually served as the central topic for one of the days on my rotation, so everyone in my rotation including me learned everything there was to know about his case. Everyone standing by my side got to learn as I did that here we had a dog with a serious, life-threatening situation, one that could only be mitigated by a feeding tube. We also learned simultaneously that my future would change drastically, in that now Cooper wouldn't be able to eat even in the abnormal, upright way he had eaten before. Now I would have to smash his food, stuff it into a 60ml syringe, and inject it directly into his stomach by way of the tube. Then, once he was fully well again, we could go back to our countertop-balancing routine, and I would get back to rolling his pills down his throat, billiards-style, inside tightly packed meatballs.

What most of the other students didn't learn, however, was that all of this came at a great cost in other ways as well. That stay in the ICU saved Cooper's life, but my bill was getting higher by the day. If I had taken the time to sit down and calculate the total cost of care over the course of my best friend's life, the number would've stretched well into five digits by that point. That ICU stay didn't help matters, as it alone cost $7,000. That number might seem like enough to make most people wonder why they would continue fighting. That's not how I felt. Granted, it did make me sick to my stomach, but only because, as an aspiring vet on unpaid clinical rotations, I didn't have seven *hundred* dollars in my bank account, let alone seven thousand. But none of that mattered. Every time Cooper smiled at me, it reinforced the conviction that I had to do whatever it took to make his life great again.

I have to do this, I thought. *I just need to figure out how to make it more affordable moving forward.*

As is the case for any twenty-something struggling with money, credit cards played a huge role in the equation. Those years buried me in so much debt, I had a hard time believing that I would ever get out of it. I never let that bother me, though, because my primary motivation was figuring out how to keep Cooper happy and healthy. The bills were considerable, given the $230-per-day average it cost to keep him in the ICU, run the bloodwork and cultures he needed, and fill his various prescriptions for antibiotics and seizure medications. It got to the point where some of the residents in the hospital—people who could easily relate to the poverty I was living under during rotations—began picking up how tough this must have been for me. I'm very fortunate that they started looking for ways to help me cut costs. The biggest money-saver was that they would find different injectables that were donated to the school and would be able to administer them to Cooper free of charge. That helped more than

I can say, as at least one of his injectable meds cost $35 per dose, and he was getting those things multiple times per day.

On top of that, some of the residents applied for a grant because Cooper was such a unique and interesting case. It took a while, but they landed it and were able to put a few thousand dollars toward lightening the load on my bill.

So it was that, through all those brilliant minds churning through the Purdue veterinary program and the goodwill of altruistic residents, Cooper came through. By the time the ordeal had reached its end, I was close to graduating. This also meant that the lease on my apartment was coming to an end. With all that had to be done to finish the program, pack my apartment, and find a place to work and start my life, I found that time grew short on having a roof over my head. Here was where that heartwarming altruism came back into play. One of the residents who had been working with me offered to let Cooper and me stay at her house until my boy could get back on his feet. Given that I graduated on January 26th of 2006 and Cooper was still in the hospital until the 31st, I had about a week to bridge until he could even leave.

It was all so hectic, I hardly even noticed my graduation day. After several years of study, it was all pretty anticlimactic. Most of the Purdue students wouldn't graduate until May, so it was just me and a couple of other Ross students who graduated in January. On top of that, I was still on rotation and had a ton of work to do. The only thing that reminded me of the day's significance was the banner someone had put up in the hall with all the graduating Ross students' names on it.

The Purdue students were excited for us, but sad to see us leave. Those of us who were leaving were still up to our eyeballs in work, and also kind of blinded by the notion that, "Oh my gosh, we're done." I had an additional layer of confusion because, while most of my fellow graduates prepared to start their careers back home or in some other part of the country, I had to hit the pause button while Cooper recovered.

I wandered around the halls that day just wondering what in the world I was going to do next. Looking to my future, I got that butterfly feeling in my stomach. Everything I had dreamed about as a kid, and everything I had worked so hard for as a twenty-something, was coming to fruition. And yet, I didn't know *when* I could actually start practicing veterinary medicine. I was stuck in limbo.

My tentative plan was to return to Pittsburgh temporarily to take the state and international boards before determining where to go next. Those were supposed to be some excruciatingly difficult exams, and the earliest I could take them was February, so I figured it was as good a plan as any. This way, I could tackle them while most of the material was still fresh in my mind. Plus, staying at home would eliminate distractions while I studied. The only problem was: when would I get to leave Purdue? When could I finally break Cooper free of this hospital and plan my next step?

It was time to start my life anew. I had just completed my dream of graduating from vet school. Now I would get to serve in exactly the role I had wanted to serve since I was a little girl.

Except I didn't have anywhere to go.

CHAPTER ELEVEN

Hoxie Pond

I didn't want to go back home. Not that I wouldn't have enjoyed crashing in my parents' basement again—my family and friends would have been a welcome comfort after the emotional rollercoaster Cooper and I had been through those last few months of school. It just felt like the time had come to start a life of my own. So without a clear direction, I did what so many young people do: I followed my boyfriend at the time.

Jay was a boy I had met at Ross. There, we had been nothing more than friends. But when we both wound up at Purdue for our clinical rotations, the friendship evolved into something more. I didn't know much about where I wanted to take my life next, but Jay thought it would be a good idea for me to move with him out to Massachusetts so we could start a new chapter in our lives together. The whole adventure was rather unexpected, and ultimately turned out a tad tumultuous. But that's young love for you, and without that journey, I'd never have met the man I would marry.

Jay and I dated for two years, moving from Purdue to Westport, Mass, and staying together through my first year as a practicing vet. I spent that year at an animal hospital in Sandwich, Cape Cod. Our place in Westport was a forty-five-minute commute to the Sandwich Animal Hospital, which was nice because those forty-five minutes there and forty-five minutes home added up to my only hour and a half in any given day where I could relax and unwind. The morning commute allowed for some coffee and an opportunity to wake up. The ride home made for a nice cooldown after what were typically pretty stressful days. On top of it all, keeping Cooper happy mattered most.

My mentor was Dr. Leslie Harmon, and I could not have asked for a better person to serve that role. She started me out on the small, simpler procedures like routine checkups, vaccines, consultations, and so on. Then she would help me out whenever I would venture into the bigger things like surgery.

I'll never forget my first surgery. I'd worked in similar situations during school, of course, but out in the real world, I discovered two important differences: first, a vet doesn't typically have the same level of assistance and guidance she might have gotten used to during vet school, and second, surgeries are significantly more difficult without that assistance and guidance.

My first solo surgery was to spay a six-month-old Golden Retriever. I remember during the process having to continually remind myself to stop looking for someone to step in and help me. A good friend of mine, a vet tech named Aleta, was in the room monitoring the anesthesia, but everything else fell to my nervous hands.

Welcome to the real world, I kept thinking.

I could not have been more nervous. I kept thinking about how I would possibly explain myself if anything went wrong. In the event of disaster, I would have to bare my soul to the poor Golden's owners, and then would have to share the failure with Dr. Harmon. That would not have made for a good day. And so, between the nerves and my determination not to let anyone down, I worked about as deliberately as anyone has ever worked on a surgery like that. It took me almost two hours, whereas a spay now takes me an average of about twenty minutes.

We came through that first surgery just fine, my first patient bouncing back quickly and happily in that typical Golden puppy fashion. Once the procedure was over, I remember feeling as if I could float right out of the room. The mix of pride and relief was unlike anything I had ever encountered before. As terrified as I had been, I knew that this feeling was something I could get used to.

This was another element of my career made easier by my experiences with Cooper. For most vets just getting their start, I suspect that the sheer magnitude of the emotional highs and lows comes as a shock. For me, though, I'd been through it all already. This isn't to say that it didn't affect me as deeply as it might have—I still laughed and cried with the best of them. It's just that I always felt more prepared to manage the emotional load.

On that front, one case that sticks out involved a nine-year-old black lab. The poor boy was diabetic and had pancreatitis. His owner, a fifty-something working mother who wore her blond hair to her shoulders, couldn't afford the frequent treatments associated with those two conditions. But she loved her dog more than anything. I'll never forget her heartbreaking looks whenever I informed her of her dog's need for another expensive treatment.

"I promise we're going to do everything we can and keep the cost low," I would tell her.

This would seem to perk up her spirits. "Thank you, Doctor Strahsmeier," she would tell me. "I just don't know what I would do without him."

And so the hospital staff and I would do as much as we could for this troubled but adorable lab with the limited resources available. With conditions like his, though, there is only so much you can do. We took him in as a critical case and allowed him to stay with us since his owner couldn't afford to take him to the emergency hospital, but we didn't have the same kinds of equipment or staff or overnight care as an emergency hospital could have offered.

One morning, I came in to check on him as I did every day, and it was clear that something had changed for the worse. He was barely responsive. I could sense that this would be his last day.

It's the toughest call a vet must make, the one to an owner, informing her that she should come in for a visit because her dog will soon die. As I made that call, I looked back at that poor lab, his cage decorated with the rosary and with the family photographs his owner was always changing out for him.

When she answered, I could hear that she was crying already. "Is he…?" she trailed off.

"No. But you may want to come in today, because I'm not sure how much time he has left."

A long silence followed before she summoned the strength to reply. "I have to work, but I'll talk to my boss and get there as soon as I can."

I told her I understood and assured her that it was okay and that we would do everything we could to keep her dog going long enough for her to come for a visit. When I hung up, I went back to her dying friend and opened his cage. He was too weak to lift his head to look up at me, so I bent down and hugged him around the shoulders. I gave him a pat, kissed him on the head, and offered a few spirited words. Then I checked his vitals one more time, adjusted his fluids, and with a heavy heart, went off to meet my first appointment of the day.

Later that morning, he was gone. As difficult as that first call had been, the second was far worse. In the moment, I somehow managed to console the lab's owner without breaking down. But then, as soon as I was alone, I found a chair in the corner and put my head in my hands, sobbing. Not only was this case near and dear to me because of how hard I had worked on it, but the lab reminded me of Cooper. Facing his mortality was emotionally difficult. It taught me the hard way what being a vet is all about. You can try to save them all, but ultimately, it's impossible. You do as much as you can for them but have to understand that it's sometimes still not enough.

Sometimes the "do as much as you can for them" is itself a harrowing experience, as well. My first euthanasia case was so crippling emotionally that I had trouble getting through the rest of the week. Staysail was the dog's name, her family being nautical by nature. She was a Golden. To see an animal that's so close to death is always a sincere reminder of one's own mortality, and the emotion is heightened when you see the animal surrounded by grieving loved ones.

Staysail was accompanied by a family of four, the two parents and two children all sobbing. This wasn't unusual. Most people who arrive for this kind of terrible occasion find it difficult to control their sorrow. There's a soft, desperate sort of sadness that hangs like a thick mist in this kind of room. It was an examination room like any other in the hospital, but in this one, at the center rested Staysail on the nice, soft, favorite blanket her family had thought to bring along. She was laterally recumbent and nonresponsive. Everyone in the family had stepped forward to pet her or gently lay a hand on her head, but still she did not move or react.

In a situation like that, stepping in as the vet is awkward. I've been on both sides of it, so I can appreciate how difficult it is for everyone involved. As emotionally close as families are with their pets, they almost always recognize the mercy in the moment—but still, it's tough to shake the hand that will help end your pet's life.

"I know this is difficult," I said on the day of Staysail's passing. Of course I could relate completely with the emotion, because I had been fearing this moment for Cooper for years by then. "But I promise it will go smoothly and Staysail will be completely at peace."

"Will there be any pain?" the father asked.

"No pain. The injection is designed to be painless." I spoke some words of encouragement and understanding to soften the blow but soon realized that nothing I could say would make this any easier. In a situation like that, the most merciful thing a vet can do is a good, efficient job. The goal can't be to tell them that everything will be okay—the goal has to be only to do it right so that the family will remember the last moments as fondly as possible.

Never mind that this was my first. Never mind the crowd in the room watching me work. What made me nervous, and what made my hands shake so hard that I had to steady myself so I could hit the vein with the syringe on the first try, was the vision of possibly having to do this to Cooper one day. I had cried my eyes out before this procedure, and I had wondered if the family could tell. When I started to brim with tears in the exam room, I tried to stop myself. *Pull it together, Katti.*

But then I remembered something a vet had told me back when I was doing my externship. "Let them see you cry," she said. "Let them know it's hard for you too. That will actually help them grieve."

This turned out to be sage advice, particularly on that first occasion. The tears spilled over my cheeks, and I could feel that poor family crying along with me. I had to stop and restart more than once, but eventually I found what I was looking for and made the injection.

Then I stepped back so the family could lay their hands on Staysail as she slipped away.

When it was over, I said what needed to be said and made the preparations that needed to be made. Then I found an empty room and let the floodgates open. When you're a little girl dreaming of helping animals feel better, the dream always ends happily. As you get older, you become aware of the occasional need to euthanize family pets, but it's never something you ponder until you have to do it for the first time. I can't say it changed my perspective on the job exactly, but it did jolt me awake to the reality that there would be grim days like this. More than that, it made me realize that I was going to have to get used to doing this, because if I didn't, I'd be crying all the time and would never make it as a vet.

Cooper, as always, proved my best medicine. Every time I had a tough time at work, I would go back to the kennel—where he stayed every day I was on the job—and give him a hug and a kiss. He always reminded me and made me appreciate what he and I had fought for, and what we still had. That's another one of those great things about dogs. If you're ever having a bad day, you can just go hug them. And they always understand.

Cooper would be there to set his head in my lap, look at me with those big eyes and that smile, and silently tell me everything was going to be all right. The mortal reality of my job was almost more than I could bear sometimes, but my dog never showed any hesitation to help me carry the load. In some respects, Cooper and I were almost always doing that for each other. He would help me through my tough days, and I would help him through his tough days. We had his seizures under control for the most part, but during that first year in Massachusetts, he ran into some pretty rotten luck. We took many trips to the local ER hospital for seizures, aspiration pneumonia, and other mishaps. On every occasion, he bounded out of the place in the way only Cooper knew how. But then there was the one trip when something went terribly wrong.

On that visit, Cooper's intravenous catheter wasn't working. Sometimes a catheter that isn't properly placed will become nonpatent, which means it doesn't work anymore due to kinking or clotting or some other unforeseen issue. Typically a tech or vet will catch this and just replace it. But on this occasion, the catheter wasn't flowing into the vein anymore, and no one noticed. When you inject a catheter in this condition, the fluid doesn't go into the vein, but to the surrounding tissue. So, when medications are injected, they can cause the skin to slough away, which will then lead to an abscess. Since they were pumping diazepam into Cooper, an abscess developed, which was particularly huge, and soon he became septic. Out of all of his brushes with death, this was the absolute closest he ever came. Blood infections are serious business, as now you're working against the clock to rebalance the poison coursing inside your dog. He was sicker than he had ever been. He lost all the skin from his ankle down. The bandaging was constant and considerable, and lucky us, it came with several more days of hospitalization, along with all the accompanying monitoring and financial commitment.

Fortunately, Cooper pulled through. And even in that sorry state, he was his old self again. But now I had to face the fact that none of this would have happened had the tech seen the signs that the catheter wasn't working. In other words, I was a vet and the loving owner of a dog, but now I had to navigate the role of a client wronged by a hospital.

It didn't help that I adored the place. Cooper came in so often that I had gotten to know everyone really well. He spent much of his time in the ICU, which resided down a long hallway broken up by several examination rooms. I always felt warm here because of the caring people I would meet, but the building itself contrasted that sentiment somewhat. The décor was drab and dreary, from the neutral walls to the light-gray tile. Not that I'm advocating for a bunch of cheeriness in a place like this—you are, after all, in this building for a drab and dreary reason.

The ICU itself was huge, with thirty or so cages and runs lined up along the walls. In the center of the room stood a rectangular island meant for examinations, and for writing charts, ordering medications, and so on. This ICU was where the tech had kept pumping diazepam into Cooper's faulty catheter. It was here that bad luck struck, and no matter how great the hospital and its staff were— and they truly were great, having done so much good for my puppy over the years—Cooper took the kind of turn for the worse that would add another week onto his stay.

Sometimes these things happen. And to the hospital's credit, they gave me a break and discounted some of the bill. But as a vet still catching up to the tremendous amounts of debt I had rung up during school and clinics, it meant having to spend even more money I didn't have.

In the end, despite this additional strain, I was overwhelmed with gratitude that Cooper had at least made it through. True to form, despite the skin loss and consequent month of bandaging, he retained that same old lust for life. Seizures, aspiration pneumonia, various run-ins with ingestion issues, and now a blood infection that nearly killed him and temporarily hobbled him, and he was still that same happy-go-lucky dog. Even today, any time I start feeling sorry for myself after a bad day, I try to remember how easy it was for Cooper to look all that difficulty in the face and just grin at it.

A whole month of changing bandages on the daily— of medications and antibiotics and a complicated healing process that would leave him with a scar, but otherwise healthy—and Cooper was still all about life.

Maybe it was that incident that made me realize I needed to be all about life too. Things weren't working out with Jay. Continuing to live together just wasn't in the cards. So Cooper and I packed up and moved to Cape Cod, where I would begin the single life for the first time since my graduation. Since I was able to have Cooper with me at work every day, and since we lived on the second floor of the building that housed the clinic, Cooper and I had the opportunity to become closer than ever. When I was working, he was right there in the dog run, and I could always go see him whenever I needed a Cooper pick-me-up. In the evenings, we would just climb the stairs to our apartment and hang out.

But the best part about our new life was the wilderness immediately behind the clinic and our apartment. To get there, we just had to lace Cooper up with his leash, step out of the building, walk about a block down the street, and then cut through on a little path that would take us into the trees. The entry to our sanctuary was a long road of sand and dirt lined on either side by thick pine trees. The path wound around and circled a cranberry bog. As if that weren't idyllic enough, there were paths leading around and in all directions away from the bog, and one of them led to what would become one of our favorite places in the world: Hoxie Pond.

Most often, we would take the path that led around the bog and to a beach on the near side of the pond. After Cooper romped around there for a while, we would continue to the far side, where another beach awaited. There was a wooded area up the hill from this spot, itself equipped with tranquil little paths, but Cooper's heart always seemed to take us to the water's edge. It made me laugh, the way he would drag me by the leash through the woods, around the bog, and to that beach. Many dogs would have been so enamored by the variety of nature in that park, but Cooper always seemed to have one goal in mind.

By the time we rounded the final bend in the path before the beach came into view, it would always be a struggle to keep up with him without stumbling over my feet. The moment we would get to the sand, I would reach out to release the leash and let him free. Then, he would take off. I mean, he would just *book it* out to the water.

He would leap from the beach and wade in to about chest level. And then, against every sense of logic or reason, he would just stand there. The water gave him so much joy, but he didn't even play in it. He would just stand there and look back at me. The whole thing was hilariously anticlimactic.

I'll never forget that image of him, though, because it's one of my fondest memories of anything ever. Cooper standing there in the water, happy as can be, smiling back at me, the pines reflecting off the crystalline water, the sunset casting orange hues into the sky and rendering the pond a metallic sort of purple. Those days were so breath-takingly perfect and beautiful, I still can't stop smiling when I think about them.

That would be a special place for Cooper and me during what was probably the most special time of our lives together. We had never been closer and would never have better opportunity to spend time in each other's company. There at Hoxie Pond, when Cooper and I would just stare at each other—his feet in the water and mine in the sand—we would experience the peace of that place together, and would understand each other in the purest, most perfect way. I loved him so deeply in those days, and in his joy, life seemed so very idyllic. He would etch himself indelibly on my heart, a mark that no amount of change or happiness or stress could ever wipe away.

• • •

Life continued in this way for months. Cooper remained happy and healthy, and I was enjoying my simple, single life in that apartment above my place of employment.

As he would in just about every place I worked, Cooper became something of a mascot at that clinic. He had such a vibrant personality, and was so beautiful besides, that the people I worked with couldn't help but adore him. His bond with that clinic became so strong, in fact, that they eventually chose him as the model for an advertisement they used in the local papers and online. The office manager at the clinic wound up soliciting a number of photos for the ad, ultimately picking a picture of Cooper in a birthday hat. I still laugh when I think about him mugging in newspapers and on websites all around the area.

Given that the clinic's purpose was to serve local pets, Cooper would be a pretty great spokes-dog in another sense as well. He was a pretty frequent client of the clinic himself. We took several trips to the hospital in those days, but he always recovered just fine, and always seemed so adorably oblivious to what a troublemaker he was in terms of his health. He wound up with inflammatory bowel disease, which led to an even more specialized diet to add to our upright feedings and meatball-administered pills. Fortunately, we adjusted quickly, but it did contribute to the sense that there would be no escaping Cooper's fate. It was almost as though the universe was content to throw shade his way all the time, but none of that darkness ever managed to penetrate his sunny disposition. So in a weird way, even though Cooper had had a run of trips to the hospital, his continued perseverance gave me a sense that everything was going to be okay after all. And yet, I had this sense of change hovering over me.

At the time, I was so focused on my career and on Cooper that I never would have guessed that the change had anything to do with me. But that's how it was. My sister Gretchen and her husband Jason had recently had their first child, Dylan, and so, on the occasion of his baptism, I traveled back home to Pittsburgh. It was February of 2008, and I couldn't have been more honored to serve as Dylan's godmother.

It was a beautiful ceremony, and my love for my nephew filled my heart, but the thing I would remember most from that day was the gaze of some handsome guy sitting amid the crowd in the pews. Of course, I kept my attention on the ceremony itself, but I couldn't deny myself the feeling I experienced when our eyes met. It was like nothing I had ever known.

At the party after the baptism, my heart practically stopped when he came up to me in the kitchen. I was so smitten that I can't remember anything about the first thing he said to me, but I did manage to gather that his name was Sam, and that he was invited to the ceremony because Jason was his best friend from high school.

Suffice to say, Sam was charming. There were many people at the party I wanted and needed to talk to, but he and I stayed at each other's sides all day and into the evening. We talked about everything: ourselves, our lives, our respective towns, that explosion of culture that was 2008, *everything*. Then, later, we played beer pong.

Since I had flown in for the weekend, I didn't have a car, which meant that I needed a ride home at the end of the night. Sam was quick to offer, and I very nearly took him up on it—in fact, I badly wanted to take him up on it—but some other friends of mine jumped in first. I decided that going against their insistence would make my attraction to Sam too obvious. So I said goodbye to a man with whom I had felt a deep connection, worried that I would never see him again. He lived in Pittsburgh, after all, and I would be heading back to Massachusetts the following morning.

But I just couldn't get him out of my head. The next few days at work, I would find myself distracted by a memory of something he had said, or of his infectious laugh. Thinking about him made me feel warm. Forget about the distance between us. Forget about how little time we had spent together and how generally little we knew each other. Who cares? I was smitten.

So I called Gretchen. We chatted for a while about how nice the ceremony and party had been, and I got caught up on all the hilarious new cooing sounds Dylan was making, but then I got down to brass tacks.

"I really liked Sam. I would date him if I lived in Pittsburgh."

For a while, she just laughed.

"What?" I said, embarrassed. "What's so funny?"

"Oh nothing. It's just that Sam said the same thing to Jason just yesterday."

I think I smiled for the next forty-eight hours straight. It turned out that, during that time, my sister and brother-in-law had decided they had to pull out all the stops to get me and Sam together. So they made up a story—a ploy, really—for me to come to their townhouse in Philadelphia, and an even flimsier excuse for Sam to make a coinciding trip in from Pittsburgh. Everyone knew what was up. Under most circumstances, that might have bothered me. But not this time. Not with Sam.

On the day I was to leave for Philadelphia, I was giddy with excitement. I set Cooper up in the kennel at the hospital, packed a too-large suitcase, and flung the thing into the back of the Four Runner for which I'd traded in the Jeep sometime after the move to the Cape. Since it was still so new, I figured I could rely on it to make the trip with no trouble. So that morning, I was surprised to meet the check engine light flashing on the dash.

"You've got to be kidding me."

I didn't know a thing about cars. Back when I lived at home, my dad took care of any issues I had with the Jeep. Then I'd been in the Caribbean and bouncing around through vet school for so long that I hadn't exactly gotten caught up on the rigors of car ownership. The Four Runner was pretty much just a means to an end. But I did know one thing: you shouldn't drive long distances in a car shining its check engine light.

"This isn't happening," I groaned.

Because I'm a cheeseball, the first thing I pictured was Sam whistling happily in his own car as he headed eastward toward Philly. He probably hadn't even left yet, but that's what I pictured. I wondered what he would think if he got all the way there, only to learn that I had decided not to come. Would he misinterpret my car trouble as an excuse not to see him? Would he lose interest in me?

Then I imagined making it halfway to my destination and getting stranded. So my first call was to my dad, who I figured might know at least a little more than I did about the problem.

"I couldn't tell you," he said simply. "I'm not sure I'd make that drive, though."

That wasn't what I wanted to hear, and my dad—being the great dad he is—clearly picked up on it. "I'll call Bill."

"Are you sure?"

"Of course. He loves talking about this stuff. He's a mechanic."

So I thanked my dad and told him I wouldn't go anywhere without his and Bill's say-so.

Then I called Gretchen.

"Hey, have you left yet?"

"No," I said, suddenly wanting to cry. "My stupid check engine light is on. I'm not sure I should come. Dad said he's going to call Bill, but I don't know."

"Wait, no," Gretchen said urgently. Then there was the sound of some shuffling, and I could hear her talking to Jason in the background. "Jason's calling Sam because he has a Four Runner too."

My heart skipped at the strange coincidence. The love-struck little girl in me wondered whether this was a sign. But the reasonable woman version of me told myself to shut up and hope it all worked out. What followed was a weird dance of Jason asking Sam a question over the phone, then relating the answer to Gretchen, who passed it on to me. It was a long game of "Telephone" featuring four actual telephones. But somehow it worked. By consulting his manual and getting the second and third-hand information through our telephone train, Sam managed to tell me what was wrong with my car. And it turned out to be basically nothing.

The moment I finished with that call, the one I'd been waiting on from my dad came through.

"Bill says it's basically nothing," Dad echoed. "I guess those lights will come on just when one of these new cars needs a software update."

"So I can go?"

"You can go."

The drive was on.

I crossed my fingers that Bill's wisdom and Sam's owner's manual were right, and cranked the car onto the road. Along the way, every time the engine made a funny noise, I would wince and prepare for the smoke-out, but it never came. The further along I got, the less stressed I felt about the car, and the more stressed I felt about making a good impression with Sam. It had been a couple months by that point, so I kept trying to riddle out whether I had remembered our meeting correctly. Had he really been as into me as I recalled? Or had I just imagined the whole thing? I tried to take solace in the idea that he wouldn't be making the long trip across the state if he weren't into me, but that didn't even work because I would always tell myself that he might be doing it out of loyalty to my brother-in-law.

My nerves peaked right around the time I pulled into my sister's driveway. By the time I got to the door, my palms were sweating. Seeing Gretchen's face when she answered the door went a long way toward calming me, but I still didn't feel quite like myself. Something about this meeting just seemed so fateful. I couldn't put my finger on it, but I just *knew*. For most of the trip, I had pictured Sam as greeting me in various ways, most of them almost courtly in their cordiality. There he was kissing my hand in one daydream. Presenting me with a rose in another. Bowing and wearing an ascot in another.

But when Gretchen stepped aside to let me in, there Sam was, just lying on the couch, his feet kicked up as he and Jason watched golf on TV. He looked up right away and smiled at me.

"Katti!"

"Hey, I didn't know you were going to be here," I said, just trying to play it off.

I gave my sister and brother-in-law hugs, then looked over at Sam, who remained on the couch. We just traded glances for a while, smiling. It seemed kind of weird to me that he didn't get up off the couch to come greet me. The moment was awkward, as I didn't know what to say or do. But then I noticed the reason that Sam hadn't exactly sprung to his feet: one of those feet was confined to a walking boot.

He seemed to notice that I was staring at his injury, because his eyes followed my gaze down to his foot. "Oh. Right. Tore my plantar fascia." He broke into a self-deprecating grin and explained the athletic but probably somewhat-less-than-athletic way he had met with the injury. "I was playing basketball with some friends, and it happened when I landed after a jump-shot."

"Oh."

"I have to wear this thing for six weeks."

In retrospect, that stupid boot wasn't the most attractive thing about him. But then, the more I thought about it, the more endearing it became. He had hurt himself only days ago but had still made the trip. He must have had good reason…

That boot turned out to be a nice icebreaker as well. It eased the mood and set us all up for some small talk and a proper hang-out.

It was a nice night, and I went to bed charmed and happy. The next day was more of the same, Sam and I sharing an effortless rapport. Our host and hostess noticed; they got back to making flimsy excuses and found a reason to leave Sam and me with Dylan for a few hours. Dylan was already in bed by then, so I guess we figured it would be okay to leave the two least experienced babysitters I could imagine in charge of the baby. Either that, or Sam and I were so intoxicated by the idea of having a couple hours alone that neither of us thought to mention that we didn't even know how to change a diaper.

"He'll sleep, though, right?" Sam said the moment it occurred to us that we were now alone in a house with a baby we didn't know how to manage.

I raised an eyebrow. "He should."

Of course he started crying right that second. The two of us spent the next hour racing around the house, fumbling with things our favorite TV shows had taught us would help appease a crying baby. I don't have any idea how we got him to calm back down to sleep, but I do know that it would've made for a good highlight reel. More importantly, it brought Sam and me closer together.

We had our first kiss that night. The electricity of it was just further proof that this was something more than either of us had ever experienced before.

The next day, a Sunday and the day we were set to head back home, we stuck around later than we might have otherwise so we could go out on a lunch date. We chose a place called Cosi, which was essentially a glorified deli, and talked about who we were and what we wanted in life. We spent a good three hours at that lunch, neither of us wanting to leave, but it only took an hour for it to become completely clear. We would have to date. It just made too much sense. Everything but the long-distance part.

So most of what we talked about was how we would make the distance thing work.

"Well, don't expect me to talk on the phone all the time," Sam said. "Because I don't like it."

That thought had disappointed me some, but when I said we would just have to figure it out, he quickly agreed.

On that front alone, things seemed bleak. But then we wound up talking on the phone every night for two, three, and four hours at a time. And despite the logistical hurdles, we visited each other every weekend. We would alternate between me traveling to Pittsburgh, him coming to the Cape, and the two of us meeting at Gretchen's in Philly. We did this every weekend for twenty-three con-secutive weekends. I wound up getting the check engine light on my car taken care of, but the mileage that followed would annihilate the poor thing. Plus, the $10,000 I spent between gas and plane tickets further destroyed my bank account.

Far more important than any of that, there was Cooper, who I hated to leave behind on weekends once or twice every month. Poor guy would usually have to stay in the kennel at the hospital whenever I would go to meet with Sam. That had proven to be a necessity for as long as Sam and I were trying this long-distance thing, though, because my one attempt to bring Cooper along had been a disaster. It was the first weekend after we had decided to date. Sam and I were obviously excited to enjoy a full forty-eight hours together, but then Cooper wound up aspirating and we had to pass most of that time in the animal hospital.

In some ways, that was when I knew for sure that Sam was the one for me. He never once complained about how much time we had to spend in that depressing place and for that depressing reason. I could tell at the time that he didn't fully understand why I kept working so hard to keep Cooper going, but he never once questioned me. That weekend turned out to be chaos, and there Sam stood by my side through it all. He would even stay with Cooper the couple of times that I had to leave on an errand or to perform some duty related to my dog's care.

So, prior to that moment, if I'd had any doubts about Sam being the one, that incident pretty much eliminated them. I loved him for being there for me. I loved him for not complaining even once about how boring and emotionally draining it is to spend hours and hours in a waiting room. And I loved him because he was so impossible to get out of my head.

Twenty-three consecutive weekends together. At some point, you have to look at the streak and realize it's a trend. We had already known pretty much since week number two that we would one day be married. So, after the twentieth week or so of traveling to see each other, we decided that there was no avoiding how much we wanted to be together. Our love for each other was so clear and so certain that it was impossible to imagine a scenario where it wouldn't work out—whether we lived on the Cape or in Pittsburgh or in Portland, Maine. Ultimately, between our shared roots in the city and the portability of my job, I decided to move back to Pittsburgh.

Before I could even start working on the logistics for how to make that happen, though, life would throw another curveball at Cooper. It would be one of the worst nights of my life. I went out to dinner that night with clients from the hospital, a great couple of people named Vicky and Doug. The two of them had offered to take me out as a thank you for how I had cared for their dog when it was sick. It was a lovely night out with my friends, but there was disaster as soon as I returned home.

It was around 9:30 when I walked through the door. Cooper was so excited to see me that he couldn't seem to control himself. He bounced around the house, knocking into furniture and tumbling into me. Then, in a fit of exhilaration, he ran into the bathroom and started drinking from the toilet. That's gross enough on its own, but the furious speed at which he drank was what most unsettled me.

"Cooper!" I hollered. "Get out of there."

He came back into the living room, his jowls dripping with toilet water. In the next few minutes, I could see that something wasn't right. He tried to lie down but didn't seem comfortable. He got up and started stretching, which was something he had never done for as long as I had known him. With every movement, it was clear to me that he just couldn't get comfortable. His stomach started expanding to the point that he looked pregnant.

As a vet, or even as a knowledgeable dog owner, there is a special kind of terror that comes from witnessing something like this. Cooper was bloating. What that meant was that he had drunk so furiously from the toilet that he had taken in air with his water, causing his stomach to expand and threaten to flip on itself. If this happened, it would put pressure on his second-largest blood vessel, which would effectively start a shockingly short clock on his time left in this world. If this happens, the only hope is a quick and desperate surgery to turn the stomach back where it belongs. For a dog, bloating is almost always deadly.

"Oh my God, he's bloating."

Immediately, I thought about that heartbreaking book *Marley and Me*. Bloating is exactly how that adorably rambunctious dog dies. That book had made me cry for about a full day after I finally put it down. Now here it was happening in real life.

Looking back on that moment, it's clear that if my situation had been any different—if I had a different job or a different apartment, or if Sam and I had decided to move in together even just a couple of weeks earlier than we did—there would've been no hope for Cooper. But as it happened, Cooper lived with a licensed veterinarian, and just as critically, his apartment was on the second floor right above an animal hospital.

He hobbled after me as I frantically led him down the stairs and into the X-ray room. Dude weighed a hundred pounds, which wasn't a whole lot less than I weighed at the time, but somehow, I managed to lift him onto the X-ray table. A couple of presses on the machine's buttons confirmed what I feared. He was bloating.

Since it was after hours, we were alone in the clinic, but now I knew I needed help, and quickly. So I called my friend and fellow vet Leslie Harmon, who lived only two minutes away.

"Can you come take a look at Cooper?"

"What's going on?"

"He's bloating."

"Oh my God." I could hear that she was already getting herself ready. "I'll be there right away."

The gratitude I felt helped calm me. This was a kind enough act on Leslie's part as it was, just coming in after business hours. But she also had kids and a husband, so her willingness to drop everything and come help us was pretty amazing. By the time she got in her car and drove over, it was about 10pm.

It didn't take her long to look at the X-ray films and confirm my fear. Typically, the response in this situation would be to outfit Cooper with a stomach tube, but we decided against it because he was so sick at this point that we decided to trocharize him. This meant threading a large catheter directly into the stomach to release pressure. It was a drastic measure, but Cooper's vitals were making it clear that we had no choice.

"Once he's stable," Leslie said, "then we get him to the car."

"Okay."

We would need to drive him to the veterinary specialist down the Cape so Cooper could have emergency surgery, and I was trying not to think about how I'd been there a million times and knew that it would take just over twenty minutes to get there.

"The trochar should buy us some time."

Cooper was showing all the signs of a dog close to death. His gums were a deep red, which meant he wasn't getting the circulation he needed. He didn't have the strength to walk. But it was just as Leslie said: implanting the catheter in his stomach would help expel some of the gas, which would take the pressure off the vein his stomach was compressing. We worked feverishly to finish the job and then transfer him to a gurney. Then we ran him to the car and piled him into the backseat.

"Good luck," Leslie called as I flung myself into the driver's seat. "He'll be okay," she added, but I could see from her mournful expression that she was afraid she would never see him again.

I drove like a bat out of hell toward the emergency hospital. My familiarity with the place would help me get Cooper where he needed to go as quickly as possible.

With one hand guiding the car through the city like a Formula 1 driver, I used the other to fumble for my cellphone and dial the hospital. The reception staff quickly transferred the call to the surgeon, who started prepping the operating room right away.

Everything was ready when we arrived. It seemed that Leslie's idea about the catheter had bought us just enough time, because Cooper was somehow still hanging on. The last I saw of him, the surgeon and his tech staff were wheeling him away through a set of double doors. He looked like an ashen, motionless lump of what less than an hour ago had been my vibrant, lively dog. The thought of that being the last time I saw him alive was difficult to bear.

I waited and waited. I paced and fretted. It took a lot of willpower not to just burst through those doors and check in on how the surgery was going. I knew I had to occupy my time somehow or I would lose my mind. So I called Sam to tell him what happened.

The heat of the phone pressed to the side of my head as I passed through the sliding doors and stepped into the relative chill of the evening is something I'll never forget. In times of stress, you cling to little details. There was the heat of my bulky, circa-2007 cellphone juxtaposed against the cold of the concrete curb on which I sat as I rang through to Sam.

"Katti," he said, knowing already that something was wrong.

I set my head in my hands. "I'm so freaked out and upset," was all I could think to say.

"But you have to think about how many times he has come out of something like this. Seriously, though. Cooper's the toughest dog alive. He'll probably outlive us all."

On any other night, I might've laughed about how completely great Sam was at saying exactly the right thing, but on that night, I couldn't stop my mind from flashing toward pictures of the worst possible outcome. I got up and paced around as Sam kept telling me that Cooper would pull through.

"But this isn't like the other times," I said. "Bloat is serious. It's what killed Marley."

"Yeah, but that was a book. This isn't a book. And Marley didn't have a vet like you to help him through."

The tears spilled over my cheeks, my mind too numb to fully process how right Sam was and how little it mattered, given the real-world odds of Cooper's survival. "I don't know," I managed.

Once again, Sam knew just how to talk me down off the ledge: get me to blather on about veterinary procedure. "Talk me through what you did."

So I started explaining everything that had transpired from the time Cooper had helped himself to some toilet champagne and my episode of crying on the curb. With every detail, I felt a little more confident, because man, we really had done everything possible to save my best friend. Sure, Marley died this way, but Sam was right—Marley didn't have me.

"See?" Sam said. "And now you've got him at the ER hospital. You know the surgeon?"

I nodded into the phone, which I immediately realized was ridiculous, but Sam seemed to sense it.

"Then he's in the best hands possible," he said. "He's going to be okay."

That did it. That's how my boyfriend managed to pull me together on one of the worst nights I'd ever had. But I still had to contend with the crazy amount of time it takes to perform the kind of surgery that was happening to Cooper right at that moment. So I kept pacing. I paced outside. I paced inside. I'd have paced on the ceiling if physics had allowed. It was a good thing that the waiting room was empty, or I'd have driven everyone else in the room completely crazy. I drove *myself* completely crazy.

Finally the doors swung open and out stepped the surgeon. At six feet and four inches, his was a formidable frame. He was almost completely bald, and nearly as husky and muscular as a grizzly bear. The sight of him might have intimidated some people, which was funny because I'd met few people nicer than him. He wore the cliché well: just like a big old teddy bear. And he was beyond smart.

"We made it," he said, that reassuring smile of his inset in his reddish-blondish, peach-fuzzy beard.

I nearly collapsed. In that moment, I realized how tense every muscle in my body had been. When it released, I felt as if I'd just finished running a marathon. Underwater. While weighed down with a jacket made of lead. Wordlessly I asked if I could go back and see him, and the surgeon nodded.

The relief at seeing Cooper stabilized was almost more than I could handle. Dozens of monitor cables snaked onto him from a series of bleeping machines lined up on every side of him. But his color had returned, and he seemed to be breathing in that same normal rhythm he always used for sleep. He looked so much more comfortable. That was the most significant thing I noticed, in fact, and one of the sights I'll always remember. It was like night and day. The way he looked was the trigger that caused all the stress to flood out of me. It had been touch-and-go all night, but Cooper had pulled through. Again. And even though he was asleep, I could tell that he would bounce back to that same old Cooper, just like always.

Thank God he's okay.

Cooper would stay in the hospital for five days after that. On more than one occasion during his stay, I pondered how ugly a fate it would have been for him to die because of a random accident after all we had endured together to keep him healthy and happy. I knew that if we hadn't been living in an apartment above a hospital, he wouldn't have made it through the ordeal. That thought gave me the slightest amount of pause about my decision to move across the state to live with Sam.

But in the end, love is a formidable thing.

CHAPTER TWELVE

Finding Cooper

It was late November of 2008. It's still stunning to think about how much and how quickly my life changed in just six months that year. I had started in that idyllic place with Cooper and the single life above the hospital, and I would end it in an even more idyllic situation living with the love of my life and my beloved dog in the city I had adored for as long as I could remember.

Fate is a funny thing, though. Just when you think you've arrived, it tends to want to test your spirits. Sam would lose his job as an attorney only two months after the move. Since that was a huge part of the impetus for my returning home rather than having him come to me, it dealt us a pretty significant blow.

We kept it going by having an absolutely awesome time sharing a city and living in the same house. Our tradition of spending our dates walking around town or on the beach at the Cape simply shifted to downtown or along the riverwalk in Pittsburgh. Now that we were in the same city, I didn't have to board Cooper every time I was with Sam, which allowed me to free up a little more emotional space, given that I didn't have to think about him all penned up in some boarding cage for a whole weekend. Up to that point, I had felt a little bad about how much chaos my life with Cooper had introduced into Sam's day to day—I mean, we had spent one of our weekend dates taking Cooper to the emergency room—so finally having both the men I loved in the same location went a long way toward calming my nerves.

Beyond that, little had changed. Sam and I still operated under the certainty that we would one day be married—we still wore those cheap, goofy little promise rings we'd bought on a whim at a store in Hyannis—and Cooper continued his tradition of being totally chill about a cross-country move. He'd recovered from his bloat incident as completely and reassuringly as he always recovered from life-threatening situations. And by then, he was heading into his seventh year of beating the neurosurgeon's projection on his expected lifespan. Dude was crushing the odds, and he looked good doing it. He still had that peg-tube in his side, but apart from that, he'd be a strong entrant into any dog show in the area. His dog show days were over, of course, but his beauty and his lust for life would never fade.

He and I also continued the tradition of spending our days together at work. I'd taken a job at a local emergency hospital, where my new employers were fine with Cooper sleeping in a kennel in the back. He'd hang out back there, and I'd go back as often as I could to check up on him or take him for walks. Just like everywhere we went, the people at work took immediately to Cooper. He had plenty of love and attention from pretty much everyone on staff.

For the most part, Cooper's health was stable. I found myself opening the logbook of his seizures a little more frequently than I had in the Cape, but it didn't seem like anything concerning—nothing a few tweaks to his medications couldn't sort out over time. He always bounced back, as ever. And boy, did he seem to like his new city and his new live-in friend Sam.

The three of us were living in my cousin's rowhouse in a city neighborhood called Observatory Hill. The house would've been unoccupied otherwise because my cousin and her husband had moved to India for a job. So we had a nice place to live, and my cousin could keep her house while abroad, a win-win all around. Plus, the house had this nice, big, fenced-in back yard. Cooper found his peace back there. He dug that yard and the freedom it afforded him with the same completeness that he had always liked the sprawling yard in St. Kitts.

The months passed into January of 2009, and as a Christmas gift to my sister Heidi, who also lived in Pittsburgh, I offered to watch the kids so she and her husband Pete could have a rare night out. This meant that I would go to Heidi's house to watch her children while Sam stayed home to hang with Cooper.

"Are you sure this is okay?" Heidi asked as she and Pete prepared to leave. She was dressed sharply and wore a lovely perfume and that glassy-eyed "I can't believe this is happening" look that most overwhelmed parents wear when faced with the unbelievable prospect of being able to blow off some steam, unfettered.

"Of course.,"

She started to repeat the rundown of the dinner and putting-to-bed process when I assured her again that all would be well. It was at that moment, before they had even left, that my phone began to ring. I'd have left it, but since it was Sam, I answered.

"Katti-I-don't-know-what-to-do-he's seizing," my boyfriend said, the sentence pouring out like one long word.

"What?"

My sister gave me a harried, concerned gaze, so I shook my head dismissively, trying to project calm. *This happens all the time,* I wanted to assure her. *No big deal.* But in my mind, I was already skittering down the slope toward terror.

"He's lying on the floor shaking," Sam said. "His mouth is open and frothing. I don't know what to do."

Of course I had told Sam many times what to do if he found himself in this situation. It came with the territory if he was going to live with Cooper and me. But hearing about a seizure and the protocol for dealing with it was one thing, and seeing the arthouse horror-film reality of an actual seizure was entirely another. He'd heard about it, but he'd never seen it, and now that he was seeing it, he was freaking the hell out.

"You have to come home."

"I'll be home as soon as I can." I forced a smile at

Heidi, whose look of worry blended right into one of disappointment.

"What-do-I-do?" Sam said frantically.

"Just make sure there's nothing around that could fall on him," I offered as calmly as I could. "And I'll be back as soon as I can."

Heidi was starting to take off her coat, and I reached out to stop her.

"I'll call Mom," I told her. "You guys still go out. I'll wait for Mom to get here, then I'll go take care of Cooper."

"He's seizing again?"

"Yeah." So much for your Christmas gift."

Somehow, I managed to simultaneously talk Sam into a sense of calm while Cooper finished seizing while also encouraging Heidi and Pete not to waste another minute of their night out. I waited until the moment their front door closed before I too started freaking out. I paced and sucked wind as I dialed my mom's number. Then, as I pressed the phone to my head and noted the alarmed look in Heidi's kids' faces, I sighed into another forced smile and told them everything was fine. "Grammy's going to come hang out with you tonight, okay?"

"Is that right?" my mom asked, having answered the call without my realizing.

"Mom, it's Cooper."

She didn't wait for an explanation. Instead, she responded just like you might expect a spectacular mother and grandmother to respond: "I'll get my coat."

In twenty minutes or so, I'd handed off the baton of babysitting and found myself in the car, careening through the twisty, hilly roads that connect the odd, nebulous web that is the greater Pittsburgh area, all the while thinking, *Well, here we go again.*

Cooper would pull through, just like always. And after that first wave of shock and panic wore off, Sam proved a good soldier throughout the ordeal, just like always. Before I knew it, it was time to celebrate yet another of Cooper's birthdays. This would be his eighth, and by then, I had almost quit marveling at how remarkable it was that he continued to check off year after year beyond the single year he was projected to live. On this occasion, the thing I marveled about most was Sam's continued affection for Cooper—a handful of a dog that he hadn't known as a puppy and couldn't possibly have bonded with on the level that I had. Over the years, most people in my life had rolled their eyes and groaned through my doting birthday parties for Cooper. Sam certainly thought I was crazy for throwing these things, but he also understood their meaning better than anyone I'd ever met. Because he knew they made me happy, he never once complained or hesitated about having to wear one of those stupid little party hats, and he always sang along to "Happy Birthday," stronger and prouder than anyone in the room not named Katti. On Cooper's eighth birthday, Sam even cut and passed out the cake.

And so it was that our proximity and our deepening understanding of each other allowed our love to grow. I was head over heels for Sam, and along with Cooper and the home we had made in my cousin's house, it started to feel like I had a proper family of my own.

Then part of that family ran away again.

I should back up.

In terms of Cooper's care, one of the best features of my cousin's house was the yard. It wasn't exactly some spectacular oasis—mostly just a tiny deck and some grass surrounded by a wooden fence with a gate that opened to an alley and garage out back.

It was that gate that proved the problem. One day, we had a visitor to help Sam with a project, and when he left, he didn't close the gate. It was a Saturday around midday when I let Cooper out, oblivious to the fact that his pen wasn't fully enclosed. An hour or so later, I had a shift at work I needed to head off to, so I went out to check on him and realized he was gone.

"Oh my God." *How long has he been gone?*

To say that I was freaking out would've done a disservice to the term "freaking out." It was like a bad flashback and a tragedy rolled into one. I was flashing back to losing him in that rough neighborhood in St. Kitts, and then losing him again on that frigid day while staying with my parents. This dog's track record of beating the odds was remarkable, but his track record of taking advantage of every opportunity to wander was, let's just say "emotionally trying."

And now I also had Sam, who liked Cooper just fine, but mostly just stressed out when I was stressed out. His anxiety only magnified my anxiety. Eventually the two of us worked our way into a panic. We rushed to our respective cars and took off in opposite directions, rolling around the neighborhood, both of us hollering our heads off for Cooper to come back. We searched the whole neighborhood, snaking outward and then back in until we met again. Then, given Cooper's track record of marathon wandering, we turned our attention to neighboring neighborhoods and neighbors of those neighboring neighborhoods. Everywhere we went, we found no sign of Cooper.

Thinking about him trapped or hurt somewhere was bad enough, but then when the hour came up when I knew he was due for his anti-seizure meds, I started to get really nervous. If he got lost in the woods and started seizing, it likely would have been the end of him, and we'd have never found him. The idea that he could just vanish from my life as a result of one misplaced gate was enough to make me feel sick to my stomach.

Finally, just as my gas tank neared empty, my phone rang. When I didn't recognize the number, I held my breath and clicked the button to answer.

"Hi, I'm calling about a dog—*pretty* dog—named Cooper," the unfamiliar voice said.

"Oh my God, thank you," I said, nearly swerving off the road from the force of my relief.

She told me the location, but even though it was the next zip code over, I wasn't all that surprised, given what I knew about Cooper's historical stats in the game of wandering.

"How is he?"

"Oh, he's fine," the woman said, sounding somewhat hesitant. "It looks like he got into a few things."

I paused, waiting for her to elaborate. I found myself

waiting for an uncomfortable amount of time. Then, just as I drew a breath to ask the question on my lips, she answered.

"He really cut up his leg. Looks like he must have gone through a lot of brush."

"Oh, no." I visualized what she was referring to. "That's just the scar from when he was septic."

That didn't seem to mean anything to her, because she was on about this weird thing sticking out of his side. "It's like this piece of plastic. I mean, it's just stuck in there. We've been trying to pull it out, but—"

"No, no!" I cut in frantically. "Don't pull it out!"

When the caller didn't get that concept either, I decided that the best course of action would be to ask her to please just keep Cooper safe and comfortable and I would come assess the situation before anyone tried cleaning him up or pulling any lifesaving implements out of his internal organs.

So I called Sam, and we rushed home, met up, got in the same car, and went out there together.

The place was an orange-brick house set down a wooded hill. It was a nice neighborhood on a block that ran past a cemetery. There was a steep drive to get down to the garage, and the moment I crested it, I saw that they had set Cooper up on the front porch, tied to a chain. There were two women sitting with them, one petting him while the other fed him something I couldn't immediately identify. Beside him rested a bowl of water that looked pretty well sloshed through by Cooper's always-sloppy tongue.

And there was my boy, happy and go-lucky as ever. Looking at him now as I exited the car, I could see how someone might mistake his appearance as belonging to a dog who had lost a battle with some prickly shrubbery. He was unfazed to see me, because the women petting and giving him treats were kind of stealing my thunder. It was like, "Oh hey, Mom. You're here." Like he'd rather just stay there. As long as I'd known him, the clearest assessment had been that he was absolutely obsessed with food and treats. If you had an endless supply of one or the other, he would never leave your side. So the truth was that he didn't care at all about my arrival because there was food to be had.

When my boy finally finished the treats gifted him by the women who had saved him, he returned to me. That was Cooper. Always wandering. But always returning to me.

CHAPTER THIRTEEN

November

As healthy and happy as Cooper had been in the months following his journey to the neighboring zip code, I allowed myself to believe that everything was going to be all right. I even paused long enough to take care of a minor personal issue I'd been putting off for too long. It was October 12th of 2009 when I finally stopped fighting the inevitable and submitted to having my wisdom teeth removed. I mention this not because the procedure was every bit as painful as I'd always been told it would be, but because it was around the time that Cooper's health took another turn.

Whether by fate or random chance, on that same October 12th, Cooper aspirated, and it was an aspiration of the terrible variety. My head still a little foggy from the wisdom teeth extraction, I rushed him to the now-familiar ER hospital in Pittsburgh. The brilliant vets set him up well, but there was no controlling Cooper's physiology.

He had a long, devastating series of seizures while under the hospital's care. As always, though, he pulled through—or at least he did so physically. After a two-week-long stay and a fresh diagnosis of ARDS (Acute Respiratory Distress Syndrome), the hospital finally released him back to me.

Only Cooper wasn't the same. I had seen lately how every time he would seize, it would take him longer to pull it back together, and every time he would aspirate, the recovery time would extend.

But my boy was still fighting, and when he was on his feet and kicking, he still had that same old sense of Cooperness. In celebration, that Halloween, I brought him to work with me in a costume, complete with a halo and frilly angel's wings. I can still picture him that day, the bounce in his step causing those silly wings to flutter. Everywhere he tramped, he'd draw a laugh. That was Cooper, bringing joy to everyone he encountered, even when he wasn't feeling all that well himself.

I can't exactly say he wasn't feeling well by the time my shift ended that day, though. He'd spent all day running and jumping around the clinic, digging in for petting sessions and trying—and often succeeding—to eat the Doritos one of the technicians had set on the counter. With as much as we'd been through on his last round in the hospital, it did my heart good to see him looking so much like his old self.

Back home that night, when the sun set and the trick-or-treaters came out, Sam and I started answering the doorbell and handing out candy to the neighborhood kids. But every time we would open the door, Cooper would get all riled up and want to get a firsthand look at the adorable costumes. Eventually it just didn't make sense to continue like that, so I let him out in the back yard to chill.

We distributed candy for another hour before shutting off the porch light and calling it a night. I went out back to call Cooper inside. The moment I laid eyes on him, I could tell that something had happened. He looked lethargic and hangdog. Dumpy, really. It was the look he always assumed when he'd aspirated.

For the first time, I felt the finances of the situation crippling me. His most recent stay in the hospital had cost me over $5,000 that I hadn't had nearly enough time to replenish. I couldn't afford to take him there again, so instead, I checked him in to my emergency hospital and set him up on oxygen. Fortunately, his seizures hadn't returned since the expensive stay downtown, but his aspiration pneumonia had spiraled out of control. I was nervous, but I figured it would be okay, just like it always was. I had this sense that if I could make it through one more night and one more shift, I'd just open up another credit card and take him back to the specialty ER.

He spent the next two days incident free, so that calmed me some.

But then it was November. The second. A remarkably warm day in November. I got myself ready to start my shift at 4pm, then left the house early so I would have plenty of time to check on Cooper. When I pulled into the lot, I felt my excitement building to a crescendo. I just couldn't wait to see him. I practically ran into the ICU, where I found him sitting quietly, looking almost sad, his cannula poking out of his nose. It was a depressing sight, Cooper not wearing his usual smile. It was what made me realize that this moment was different.

Even with everything Cooper and I had been through together, and everything he had endured health-wise, nothing much had changed about his magnetic personality since that day I first met him and fell in love. He had the bald spots from the IV catheter and the cannula, but mostly he was still the dog I'd always known. He had that same sweet face, that same wouldn't-hurt-a-fly demeanor, and those same clumsy paws. Really, for anyone unaware of his mountainous veterinary file, he'd have probably seemed like a dog that only recently fell on hard luck. The truth, of course, ran much deeper than that.

But now he looked different. I opened his cage, disconnected his oxygen, and led him outside. The hope was that being in the sun with me would revive him some.

We wandered around a long strip of grass outside the hospital. This had become part of our daily routine even long before his health had started to take a turn for the worse. But his movements only confirmed my fears. He was slower, more hesitant, and far quieter than usual. Most days, even during his periods of recovery from the pneumonia, he would bound outside—clamoring for the fresh air and open sky, practically dragging me along behind him—but on that day, he just seemed to want to sidle up next to me and sit.

"Cooper, what's wrong, sweetheart? Are you okay?"

He looked up at me with one of those big, sloppy, wildly infectious smiles of his. His eyes said, "What?

Me? Nothing. Nothing's wrong." Even with everything we'd been through together over the years, it was rare for Cooper's eyes to say anything else. Then, he smiled a smile that said he was just happy to be there with me, like always. No matter what, Cooper loved his mama.

Between my experience as a vet and my close bond with him, I always picked up on the littlest things. Even if it were something as simple as a strange gaze, I could sense that not all was right with Cooper's world. I just knew him inside and out, instinctively and instantaneously, and on a level that I hadn't previously thought possible.

"You want to go back inside?"

He climbed to his feet and lumbered into the lead. As I watched him walk, I thought about how he used to steal my flipflops back when we lived in St. Kitts. With the salty, sun-splashed Caribbean as his backdrop, he'd snatch one of them up and tear around the pasture with it in his mouth, tossing it in the air and chasing after it like he was engaged in some deranged, solo game of fetch. I thought about how he would trot around with sticks that weighed almost as much as he did. I thought about our frequent walks along the trails at Hoxie Pond back on Cape Cod, and how he would wade knee-deep into the water and then just stand there looking back at me like he was waiting for me to join. I thought about that angel costume I dressed him in on Halloween just two days prior.

As I thought about all that, I listened to the sound of Cooper's labored breathing and couldn't help the anxiety that caused me to start shaking. When he fell back and struggled to keep up, I felt sick to my stomach. I'd spent most of my dog's life fretting about how I'd been told he wouldn't live past a year, but he was always a fighter. Here he was eight years old and probably the world record holder in vet visits, but I could tell something was different this time. No matter what fresh hell life threw at him, he had always pulled through before, but this time—

"Coopie, if you can just hold on until my break," I said, sniffling, "then I'll take you to the specialty ER, okay? You just have to hold on."

In saying it, I was ignoring my instinct to just run out of the place with him. But my nerves and fears were so overwhelming that the only thing I could do was try to get back to work and pretend this wasn't happening.

Through it all, he picked his head up to smile back at me in that reassuring way of his. The complexity of a dog's emotional range is difficult to describe, but with Cooper, the truly remarkable thing was that he was both compelled to, and capable of, pretending that nothing was wrong.

When we reached the door, I pulled myself together just enough to get Cooper in through the side door and outfitted in a stainless-steel oxygen cage we kept in the clinic's ICU. Before I closed him in, I gave him a kiss on the head and told him I loved him and that I would be right back. Then, my heart heavy, I went to work on a walk-in patient named Buster who looked very much like he was a candidate to see a specialist somewhere downtown.

My love for animals has always been a driving spirit. But on that day in November, I had to fight to focus on the dog who was whimpering on the examination table because I was so tuned in to the sound of Cooper's labored breathing from the oxygen cage on the other side of the room. Every time I looked over at him, he would give me one of those smiles, but I could tell he was tired. His eyes were droopy, and his face looked worn.

When he erupted into a violent cough, it grabbed my attention. He coughed up a large glob of reddish fluid that splashed the bottom of his crate. I rushed over and opened the door. The red of the fluid suggested a tinge of blood that stood in stark contrast to the light-green tile of the floor. My hands began shaking, but Cooper just looked up at me and smiled. He was beautiful. Always beautiful. My oversized beagle with a carriage pretty enough to win him more than one dog show back in the day.

"Can you handle Buster for a minute?" I asked the tech still holding our friend on the examination table.

With concern in her eyes, she nodded. She, like everyone else in the clinic, had come to think of Cooper as something of a mascot. I wasn't the only person in the building who loved him.

"Are you okay, Coop?"

He closed his mouth long enough to listen.

For the second time that day, I gave him a kiss on the head and told him I loved him. My heart remained with Cooper as I returned to the examination table to help our waiting patient.

Cooper bellowed into a cough for the second time. When I turned to see what had happened, I felt myself go numb. My best friend was slumped over in his cage. A large pool of that same rosy fluid expanded across the tile.

"Cooper!"

I rushed to him and pulled him out of the cage. He'd gone completely limp, but I managed to lift all one hundred pounds of him and carry him back to the table.

"Somebody help!" I heard myself calling.

I'm sure there were other technicians around me in a flash, but with my first love dying on the table in front of me, I couldn't see anything but what had to be done. Cooper's breathing had stopped, and he was nonresponsive. Reflexively, I fitted him with an endotracheal tube and started CPR. Other hands worked quickly on either side of the table. Someone set him up with a heart monitor. Someone else hooked up his tube to oxygen.

"Mama's here, Cooper," I kept saying. "Mama's here. I'm right here."

If you've never been around a dying animal, the compulsion isn't one that you might expect. You want nothing more than to assure him he isn't alone. So as the others worked, I sat there petting him and trying to look into his eyes to get some sort of response.

"Mama's here, Cooper."

We got his heart rate back, but it was weak.

I caught a glimpse of Dr. Wayne Sisk, the vet who had been on staff that morning, getting ready to leave his shift and head home.

"Wayne!"

When he didn't hear me, the technician ran and got him. It took only a moment of explanation before he rushed back and started CPR.

"You should take a breath, Katti," Wayne said, and he was right.

So I backed away into the hall, my mind reeling. My first instinct was to call Sam. The phone rang and rang. When I tried him again, it was the same. Then a third time. Still nothing. So I called my boss.

"Hey, I'm leaving," I said the moment there was an answer. "Cooper's crashing."

She replied with her sympathies, but I didn't hear much because I couldn't think about anything but the words I'd just spoken. It seemed so unreal.

"Can you come in and see the rest of my patients for me?" I asked, my eyes brimming with tears.

She agreed, so I tried Sam again. Still nothing. Once more, and nothing. I'd lost count of how many times I'd tried to call him in the span of three minutes, but I just couldn't stop myself. I knew I needed someone to be there with me in the event that things went the way they looked like they were going. But Sam wasn't there.

My own heart pounded in my chest as I ran back to Cooper and cradled his head in my arms. Through the stethoscope, I could hear the slow, faint thumping of his heart. He was stable, but I knew we were running out of options to care for him here.

"We have to get him to the specialist."

Suddenly there was Sharon, a pretty, dark-haired technician with tattooed arms and a bit of an attitude. For all the times we'd butted heads, I loved her dearly in that moment. She scooped Cooper's hind end into her arms and helped me carry him through the same side door we'd just entered after our walk.

"I'll bring your car around," Wayne said. In addition to his skill as a vet, Wayne was a good friend, and always quick to a joke that could provide some calm, so I was glad to know he would be with us for the drive.

When Wayne had the car, Sharon helped me get Cooper in through the tailgate. I slid in after him, kneeling to Cooper's right and cradling his head while Sharon climbed in near his hind end and set up with a satchel of ambulatory drugs.

"We have to hurry," I pleaded.

Wayne threw it into drive and took off. As we bounced around in the cargo space, I ran my hand over Cooper's forehead. His eyes were shut tight, but his chest still rose and fell as he labored for breath. We were three quarters of the way to downtown Pittsburgh and the waiting specialty hospital when he started to flatline again.

"I need epi!" I heard myself screaming.

Sharon produced the epinephrine, and I didn't hesitate to inject it into Cooper's heart. He returned to me then, but I knew time ran short, and we still had traffic ahead. As Wayne picked his way over the Fort Pitt Bridge, moving toward the city's skyline, I had trouble keeping Cooper from sliding around in the backseat.

We didn't have far now. Just an exit and several stoplights I prayed would be green. But before we even reached the exit, Cooper flatlined again.

"Another!" I called to Sharon, who handed over another round of epinephrine.

For a second time, I somehow managed to find my best friend's heart despite the jostling in the backseat, and for the second time, it revived him. We had made the exit, and I could see the string of lights we would have to clear up ahead. All of them were green.

Cooper's heart slowed for a third time.

The lack of sound through my stethoscope was so loud, it echoed in my head. In a single moment, I understood why I had done all this. Why I had fought to keep Cooper going. Why I had sacrificed so much of my life and my finances and dedicated so much of my love to what many people might have considered a lost cause. I just wanted to make Cooper as happy as he always made me. Selfishly, I wanted him to live, but more than anything, I wanted him to live *well*. He deserved it. His zest was unparalleled. Every smile he had ever evoked from someone else should have been delivered back to him in the form of months and years of healthy, happy living. My desperation to give that to him would stay with me at least until the moment when all hope was lost.

So there we were, flying through downtown Pittsburgh late at night in the back of my car, epinephrine in my hand, the muscles in my arms screaming with exhaustion from the CPR.

It's impossible to describe the sorrow one feels when that final thread of hope falls away—that moment when you realize you've done everything you could do, and it just wasn't enough. It's like falling down a deep well, falling so far that you're certain you'll die when you make impact, but not caring in the slightest if you die because what does it matter if you've failed the one you loved?

"His heart stopped," I said.

Sharon had already drawn up the epinephrine and handed it to me one last time.

"Stop," I said in a voice just above a whisper, more to myself than to Sharon.

I looked at her, and she gave a teary-eyed nod.

"Just stop," I repeated. "We just have to let him go."

It was the day I always knew would come—the day that any dog owner knows is inevitable. But there is something about the love of a dog that forces you to think about them as if they'll live forever, even if you know they are destined to die long before you are, and even if they've been given a dire diagnosis at a very young age. Cooper had outlived his projection by eight-and-a-half years, and we had fought tooth and nail for his health and happiness all the while. The joy he had brought to me and to others during that span was immeasurable. And as his fight reached its end, I could only hope he knew how much I loved him.

I leaned down and gave him a kiss on the head. It was warm, but he was still. He was gone.

We made it to the hospital shortly after. The surgeon who owned the practice came running out to meet us, but Wayne told him softly that Cooper was dead on arrival. I knew that it was true—had felt it with my own hands and seen it with my own eyes—but it still leveled me to hear someone say it out loud.

I remember following like a ghost as they strapped my best friend to a gurney and wheeled him inside. They took him to a private room off the ER, a solitary space with dim lighting and a soft place to lay my departed friend. I stayed with him there for a long time before finally accepting that it was time to do all the things you're supposed to do when someone you love passes away.

My first call was to Sam. Actually, it was my twenty-seventh call to Sam that day. Eventually we would manage to connect, but for whatever reason, he wasn't able to pick up at the time. So instead, I dialed my parents.

"Mom, it's Cooper.,"

She had heard these three words from me many times before, but she also knew the nuances of my voice well enough to recognize that this time it was different.

"What do you need?"

I explained what had happened and why I needed her. She didn't hesitate to say that she would get my dad and meet me at the emergency hospital. When I hung up, it was as if everything inside me had shut down, and the room had gone black.

CHAPTER FOURTEEN

Hoxie Pond Revisited

I don't know how many hours it was before I finally allowed myself to leave. My parents had come and gone, as had Wayne and Sharon, and now it was just me and Sam in that little room with Cooper.

Finally it got to where the techs had no choice but to come and take him away, and I just couldn't fight it anymore.

On the day I first brought Cooper home when he was a puppy, the first time I had to leave him, I kissed him on the head and said, "I love you. I'll be right back." This had seemed to comfort him then, just as it did during the hundreds or maybe even thousands of times I had spoken the words to him over the course of his eight-and-a-half years of life. So as the techs prepared his body, I leaned in and kissed him on the head one last time.

"I love you," I said. "I'll be right back."

With my mind on some distant, painful plane, I

allowed Sam to lead me out of the ER and to his car. There was some conversation about what would happen next, but I couldn't really participate, from the burden on my heart. Eventually the message got through that Sam thought I should eat something, since it had been hours since we first set out for the ER.

Hunger seemed like such a foreign concept, but absently I agreed to let him take me somewhere to get some food. I'll never forget that the somewhere wound up being TGI Friday's. The manufactured peppiness of that place stood in such stark contrast to how I felt. Sam comforted me as well as he could from across the booth, and he ordered a ton of food, but I couldn't stop crying long enough to eat anything. We must have looked a strange— if not *alarming*—sight, the two of us sitting across from each other, Sam all big-eyed concern as I sobbed over a plate of uneaten Jack Daniels chicken strips.

I don't remember how we got home, or how my car managed to make its way back from the vet hospital, but there we were, my arm slung over my future husband's shoulder as he guided me into the living room to be alone. I sat on the floor in the corner, crying harder than I'd ever cried. The guilt I felt was like a cold wind whipping over an ocean of sorrow that came at me in waves.

The question kept hitting me: had I done enough? As Cooper's friend, could I have done anything more that could have prolonged his life and kept him healthier? Could I have made different choices as a veterinarian, both during the course of his life and in those last few moments in the car?

I never should have taken him to my hospital, I kept thinking. *I should have just called out of my shift and taken him straight to the criticalist.*

Eventually, after nearly a week of grieving, and as chilling as the guilt had been, my heart warmed all at once when a peaceful realization struck me. People love their dogs dearly, even though they know that death is inevitable. Just like I had done, people take care of their beloved dogs as much as they can in an effort to make them happy and keep them at their sides for as long as possible. But it is always a losing battle. All you can do is everything you can.

Anyone who has ever cherished a pet as a member of the family has faced the question before. $2,000 for a vet bill here, or another $5,000 to save his life there. These are the pains we take to keep our friends with us. By the end of Cooper's own veterinary saga, his bills came to more than $85,000 in total. It's a staggering number, but the truth is that I'd have spent far more than that if it had meant getting to enjoy even a little more time with my happy-go-lucky puppy.

Along the way, when his seizures started, when his aspirating began, and when food or his wandering sense of smell led him into various mishaps that only complicated his veterinary care, I managed his overwhelming daily regimen as if it were just a normal part of dog ownership. Where other people thought I was a little nutty for taking on all these tasks required to keep him healthy and happy, I saw them as something that only enhanced our bond. He'd have done anything for me, and I thought of it as nothing short of a vow that I should do the same for him.

So that was when I buried my guilt, that moment when I realized that I had done everything I could. There was all that credit card debt and all the time spent organizing his pills and standing him upright to eat softened food, and I would always be there by his side during all thirty-five of the seizures he would have during any given forty-eight-hour period. I mean, who forces her friends and family to help her celebrate her dog's birthday in the form of a huge party complete with cake and singing every year? Who takes their dog to work with them every day so she can make sure he's okay? Who performs CPR on their dog in the cargo section of a moving SUV? Who sticks their dog's heart with epinephrine to stave off cardiac arrest? The fact was, I had celebrated his life completely and had fought for him to the bitter end.

I loved this dog whose presence by my side could calm any anxiety I've ever experienced. This dog who made more messes than any human being should be able to endure with a smile. This dog who taught me more about veterinary medicine than I ever learned in a textbook. This dog whose beauty was so disarming that he once got me out of a speeding ticket. This dog who could spark so much change in my life, who could inspire me to better myself just as easily as he could cause me to throw all common sense out the window, who could teach me about who I was and who I would one day become.

Cooper was so much more than a dog to me. He was a best friend. A teacher. A mentor in the ways of love.

An inspiration for me to be a better dog owner, a better friend, and to keep going in my studies and become the veterinarian I wanted to be.

These are the many reasons why, even after all that crying, and even after these years of living without him by my side, I still think of Cooper every day. I remember him not as a dog plagued by seizures or troubled by rotten luck with his health. I remember him as one of the funniest, silliest, most loving dogs I've ever met.

Whether it was because he was the first pet I ever had on my own, or because he was so perfect and warm and selfless, we shared a special bond. It was something like the bond between mother and child, yes, but it was also something almost supernatural. The odds of the two of us leading that life together are startling to think about. Here in Cooper, you had this unique, beautiful spirit that just happened to need an unbelievable amount of veterinary care. In me, you had an aspiring veterinarian willing to do whatever it took to reciprocate the love and devotion of a special, sweet, and funny dog. Because of that relationship, a lovely soul that was supposed to die inside his first year of life wound up living eight-and-a-half years. And during those years, that same soul taught me more than I could have imagined about pet ownership, about how to be a good veterinarian, and in the end, about love.

The first time I returned to Hoxie Pond after Cooper's death, I brought a plaque bearing his name and set up a memorial for him on the shore. When I was finished, I smiled at the memory of my best friend standing perfectly still in the water as he looked back at me, his tongue hanging out and adoration in his eyes. The thought warmed me with the certainty that wherever Cooper is now, he's happy and full of life. There are no seizures and no pills. Every moment is like the shade of an avocado tree, and he's always free to wade into a pond just like this one. That is how I choose to remember Cooper. That is how he is always with me.

S hortly after Cooper passed away, Sam and I became engaged. We were married seven months later. We would share our first house as a married couple with a new cat named Buddy. Coincidentally, Buddy also hailed from St. Kitts, like Lia before him. He became a part of our family after I attended a veterinary conference on the island and decided to bring him home.

My career as an emergency vet ended around this time, when I began working for a small animal clinic and a few shelters, including a stint with the Humane Society. I fell in love with many dogs at these shelters, but one in particular caught my eye. Pepper looked so very much like Cooper that I couldn't help but adopt him. To those who say that your next dog will have a little of your old dog in him, you are exactly right. Pepper shared so many of Cooper's best qualities, and we were fortunate that he didn't share all the health problems.

Eventually, with our growing menagerie of pets, Sam and I began to nurture a dream of opening an animal hospital of our own. BelaCoop Animal Hospital of North

Park—so named for "Bela," Sam's beloved dog who passed away, and Cooper, my first love and best teacher—opened in July of 2013. When you first enter the hospital, you're greeted by a large painting of Bela and Cooper. The lobby's chairs feature pillows with their names and pictures, and on the wall hang their stories. Soon after opening the hospital, we adopted another cat named Kitniss and rescued a Pitbull named Zenny.

In 2015, I became pregnant with our first child. Within days of this being confirmed, my sister Gretchen became ill and was diagnosed with Acute Myeloid Leukemia (AML). She passed away five months later. Our baby was born the next month—a girl...just what Gretchen had wanted. We named her Siena Jaine Gretchen Stoller. Soon we decided that Siena needed a sibling. Fifteen months on, we welcomed Rainer Graham Stoller to the family.

In the years since opening BelaCoop, we have hired two associates and grown our staff from four to twenty-three. We have expanded the business to incorporate a grooming facility, and soon, a boarding facility. We hope to continue to grow so that we might serve more of the animals in our community, and so that more people will get to know Cooper's story. He was one special dog—my emotional rock during a tumultuous time of my life, my one-dog support group as I studied to become a veterinarian, and the best inspiration anyone could ask for, particularly when taking the leap to open an animal hospital. But I am most grateful for Cooper's role in making me realize how much I love Sam Stoller, and how happy I am to call him my husband and the father of our two amazing children.

Cooper taught me so much about veterinary medicine, and at least indirectly, he has taught many of my colleagues as well. Some still come to me for advice about seizure or megaesophagus cases. In this way, his life and his medical issue have made a lasting impact not just on my career but on the careers of others in the field. My family and the many friends mentioned in this book (all of whom remain great friends to this day) still smile and laugh along with me as we talk about Cooper in amazement. "Only Katti would care for a dog like Cooper in the way she did," is the general sentiment. It's almost as if Cooper and I were meant for each other.

While I didn't realize what he was teaching me and showing me at the time, when I look back, I see that Cooper fulfilled me at that point in my life. He made me a better person and a better veterinarian. I loved that beautiful dog. He will always be a part of me and everything I do.

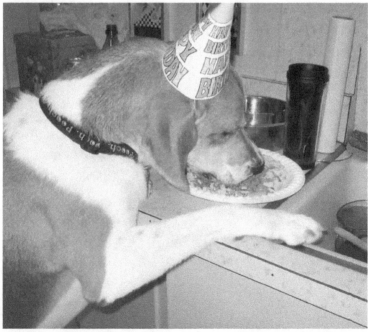

From the time she was seven years old, Katti Stoller wanted to be a veterinarian. Some of her earliest memories are of helping her dad take care of the beagles he bred and raised. The dream became a reality by way of bachelor's and master's degrees from Virginia Tech and her doctorate in veterinary medicine from Ross University on the island of St. Kitts.

She spent the first years of her career at Sandwich Animal Hospital on Cape Cod before moving on to work in emergency veterinary medicine in her hometown of Pittsburgh, PA. Later, while contributing her time to the Humane Society, she began building a private practice with her husband Sam.

BelaCoop Animal Hospital of North Park opened in July 2013. The name honors Sam's dog Bela and Katti's dog Cooper. The practice opened with only three employees but has grown to twenty employees and two other doctors. A grooming facility, BelaCoop Beauty Bar, opened in March 2019, with plans for a boarding facility called BelaCoop Bed and Biscuit to open in 2021.

Katti and Sam have two children, Siena and Rainer; two rescue dogs, Pepper and Zenny; and two rescue cats, Lia and Kittniss. When she's not at BelaCoop, you can find Katti out walking her dogs and/or spending time with her family in Pittsburgh, PA.